# Table of Contents

Introduction

# Introduction

Your roof is your home's first line of defense against the elements. It's the unsung hero that stands between you and the forces of nature, working tirelessly to keep you and your loved ones safe and dry. But like any hero, your roof needs your support to continue its vital mission.

Imagine waking up in the middle of the night to the sound of dripping water. You turn on the light and discover a growing stain on your ceiling. Your heart sinks as you realize your roof has failed you. The damage isn't just unsightly; it can lead to mold growth, structural issues, and decreased property value. The consequences of neglecting your roof can be devastating.

That's where this book comes in. "How to Install and Repair Roofing" is your comprehensive guide to becoming your roof's sidekick. With step-by-step instructions, helpful illustrations, and expert tips, you'll learn how to tackle common roofing problems like a pro. From replacing damaged shingles to installing flashing and maintaining proper ventilation, this book will give you the knowledge and confidence to keep your roof in top shape.

But we know what you're thinking: "I'm not a roofing expert. Can I really do this myself?" The answer is yes! While some roofing tasks are best left to professionals, many maintenance and repair projects are well within the reach of DIY enthusiasts. This book will help you determine when you can handle a job yourself and when it's time to call in the cavalry.

Don't wait until you're knee-deep in water to start thinking about your roof. Take a proactive approach and arm yourself with the knowledge to prevent disasters before they strike. Your roof works hard to protect you; now it's time to return the favor. Invest in "How to Install and Repair Roofing" and become the hero your home deserves.

# Chapter 1
# Roofing Materials and Tools

## Types of Roofing Shingles: Asphalt, Wood, Metal, and More

When it comes to roofing materials, shingles are the most common choice for residential homes. Shingles come in a variety of materials, each with its own set of advantages and disadvantages. In this section, we'll dive deep into the world of roofing shingles and explore the pros and cons of asphalt, wood, metal, and other popular options.

**Asphalt Shingles:**
Asphalt shingles are the most popular choice for residential roofing, and for good reason. They are affordable, easy to install, and come in a wide range of colors and styles. Asphalt shingles are made from a fiberglass or organic mat base that's coated with asphalt and topped with ceramic granules. The granules provide added protection against UV rays and help to extend the life of the shingles.

There are three main types of asphalt shingles:
1. 3-tab shingles: These are the most basic and economical option. They have a uniform, flat appearance and are designed to look like three separate shingles when installed.
2. Architectural shingles: Also known as dimensional or laminate shingles, these have a more textured and layered appearance that mimics the look of wood or slate. They are thicker and more durable than 3-tab shingles.
3. Premium shingles: These top-of-the-line asphalt shingles offer the highest level of durability and aesthetic appeal. They come in unique shapes and sizes and often feature enhanced protection against wind, hail, and algae growth.

7

Pros:

- Affordable
- Easy to install and repair
- Wide range of colors and styles
- Good fire and wind resistance

Cons:

- Shorter lifespan compared to other materials (20-30 years)
- Can be vulnerable to damage from extreme weather
- Less energy-efficient than some other options

**Wood Shingles and Shakes:**
Wood shingles and shakes offer a rustic, natural look that many homeowners find appealing. They are made from cedar, redwood, or pine and are cut to create either a smooth, tapered shingle or a more rugged, textured shake.

Pros:

- Attractive, natural appearance
- Good insulation properties
- Can last up to 30-50 years with proper maintenance
- Environmentally friendly and biodegradable

Cons:

- More expensive than asphalt shingles
- Require regular maintenance to prevent rot, warping, and insect damage
- Not fire-resistant unless treated with a special fire retardant
- Can be difficult to install and repair

**Metal Roofing:**
Metal roofing has gained popularity in recent years due to its durability, energy efficiency, and sleek appearance. Metal roofs can be made from steel, aluminum, copper, or zinc and come in a variety of styles, including standing seam, corrugated, and metal shingles.

Pros:
- Long lifespan (50+ years)
- Excellent fire, wind, and impact resistance
- Energy-efficient (reflects heat and helps to reduce cooling costs)
- Lightweight and easy to install over existing roofing
- Low maintenance

Cons:
- More expensive than asphalt shingles
- Can be noisy during rain or hail
- May dent or scratch from heavy impacts
- Requires specialized knowledge for installation and repair

**Other Roofing Materials:**
In addition to asphalt, wood, and metal, there are several other roofing materials to consider:

1. Tile: Clay or concrete tiles offer a distinctive, Mediterranean look and excellent durability. However, they are heavy, expensive, and require a specialized installation process.

2. Slate: Natural slate is a premium roofing material that can last up to 100 years or more. It offers a sophisticated, upscale appearance but is also very heavy and expensive.

3. Synthetic slate and tile: These materials mimic the look of natural slate or tile but are lighter, more affordable, and easier to install.

4. Built-up roofing (BUR): This commercial roofing system is made from layers of bitumen and reinforcing fabric and is topped with a layer of gravel or mineral granules.

5. Rubber membrane: EPDM (ethylene propylene diene monomer) and TPO (thermoplastic polyolefin) are single-ply rubber membranes commonly used on low-slope or flat roofs.

When choosing a roofing material, consider factors such as your budget, the style of your home, the climate in your area, and your long-term goals for your property. Each material has its own unique benefits and drawbacks, so it's important to weigh your options carefully and consult with a professional roofing contractor if needed.

In the following sections, we'll explore the tools and equipment needed for roofing installation and repair, as well as the important safety considerations to keep in mind when working on your roof. By the end of this chapter, you'll have a solid understanding of the various roofing materials available and be better prepared to tackle your roofing projects with confidence.

# Flashing Materials: Copper, Aluminum, and Galvanized Steel

Flashing is a crucial component of any roofing system, as it helps to seal and protect vulnerable areas where the roof meets walls, chimneys, vents, or other protrusions. Proper flashing installation is essential for preventing leaks and ensuring the long-term integrity of your roof. In this section, we'll explore the three most common flashing materials: copper, aluminum, and galvanized steel.

**Copper Flashing:**
Copper is a premium flashing material known for its durability, longevity, and attractive appearance. It is an excellent choice for high-end residential and commercial roofing applications.

Pros:
- Extremely durable and long-lasting (can last up to 100 years or more)
- Resistant to corrosion, weathering, and UV damage
- Malleable and easy to shape around complex roof contours
- Develops an attractive patina over time
- Compatible with most roofing materials, including asphalt shingles, wood shakes, and tile

Cons:
- Expensive compared to other flashing materials
- Requires specialized skills and tools for installation
- Can be prone to theft due to its high scrap value

Installation Tips:
- Use a thickness of at least 16 ounces per square foot for optimal durability
- Apply a clear sealant or coating to slow the development of patina, if desired

- Use mechanical fasteners (clips or screws) rather than solder to allow for expansion and contraction
- Avoid using copper flashing with aluminum or steel roofing, as it can cause galvanic corrosion

**Aluminum Flashing:**
Aluminum is a popular choice for flashing due to its affordability, versatility, and resistance to corrosion. It is suitable for a wide range of residential and commercial roofing applications.

Pros:
- Lightweight and easy to work with
- Resistant to rust and corrosion
- Less expensive than copper
- Available in a variety of colors and finishes to match different roofing materials
- Can be painted to blend in with surrounding surfaces

Cons:
- Less durable than copper (lifespan of 20-50 years)
- Can be prone to denting or damage from impacts
- May crack or become brittle over time due to exposure to extreme temperatures

Installation Tips:
- Use a minimum thickness of 0.019 inches for residential applications and 0.024 inches for commercial applications
- Apply a coat of bituminous paint or sealant to the underside of the flashing to prevent corrosion
- Use compatible fasteners and sealants to avoid galvanic corrosion
- Avoid using aluminum flashing with copper or steel roofing, as it can cause galvanic corrosion

## Galvanized Steel Flashing:

Galvanized steel is a cost-effective and durable flashing material that offers excellent protection against rust and corrosion. It is commonly used in both residential and commercial roofing applications.

Pros:
- Strong and durable (lifespan of 20-50 years)
- Resistant to rust and corrosion due to the protective zinc coating
- Less expensive than copper or aluminum
- Compatible with most roofing materials, including asphalt shingles, wood shakes, and metal roofing

Cons:
- Heavier and more difficult to work with than aluminum
- Can be prone to rusting if the protective zinc coating is damaged or worn away
- May not be as visually appealing as copper or colored aluminum

Installation Tips:
- Use a minimum thickness of 26 gauge for residential applications and 24 gauge for commercial applications
- Ensure that the flashing is properly lapped and sealed to prevent water infiltration
- Use compatible fasteners and sealants to avoid galvanic corrosion
- Apply a coat of rust-inhibitive paint to any exposed cut edges or scratches in the zinc coating

When selecting a flashing material for your roofing project, consider factors such as your budget, the style of your home or building, the roofing material being used, and the climate in your area. Each material has its own advantages and disadvantages, so it's essential to choose the one that best suits your specific needs and priorities.

Proper flashing installation is critical for ensuring a watertight and long-lasting roofing system. If you are unsure about your ability to install flashing correctly, it is recommended to consult with a professional roofing contractor who has experience working with your chosen material.

In the next section, we'll discuss the essential tools and equipment needed for roofing installation and repair projects, as well as important safety considerations to keep in mind when working on your roof.

# Essential Tools for Roofing Installation and Repair

Having the right tools is crucial for successfully completing any roofing installation or repair project. Using the proper equipment not only makes the job easier but also ensures the safety and quality of the work. In this section, we'll go over the essential tools you'll need to tackle a wide range of roofing tasks.

**Safety Equipment:**

Before discussing the tools needed for roofing work, it's essential to prioritize safety. Roofing can be dangerous, so always wear the following protective gear:

1. Sturdy, non-slip work boots
2. Hard hat
3. Safety glasses or goggles
4. Work gloves
5. Fall protection harness and anchors (for steep roofs or when working near the edge)

**Tear-Off Tools:**

If you're replacing an old roof, you'll need to remove the existing roofing materials first. These tools will help you efficiently tear off the old shingles and prepare the roof deck for new roofing:

1. Roofing tear-off shovel or spade: A specially designed shovel with a serrated edge that makes it easier to pry up old shingles and nails.
2. Pry bar: A long, flat bar used to remove stubborn nails and flashing.
3. Hammer: A claw hammer is useful for pulling out nails and prying up shingles.
4. Roofing knife or utility knife: Used for cutting shingles and roofing felt.
5. Roofing fork: A tool with a long handle and forked blade, used for scraping off old roofing material and debris.

## Installation Tools:

Once the old roofing is removed, you'll need these tools to install the new roofing materials:

1. Roofing nailer or nail gun: A pneumatic tool that drives roofing nails quickly and accurately. Ensure you have the correct nails for your specific roofing material.

2. Hammer tacker: Used to secure roofing felt or underlayment to the roof deck.

3. Chalk line: A tool for creating straight lines on the roof deck to ensure even shingle placement.

4. Roof snake or shingle hoist: A conveyor-like tool that helps you easily transport shingle bundles up to the roof.

5. Shingle cutter or roofing blade: A specialized blade designed for cutting shingles to size.

6. Tin snips: Used for cutting metal flashing and drip edge.

7. Caulking gun and roofing cement: Used to seal around flashing and in areas prone to leaks.

## Flashing Tools:

Proper flashing installation is key to preventing leaks. These tools will help you secure and seal flashing around chimneys, vents, and other roof penetrations:

1. Aviation snips or metal shears: Used for cutting flashing material to size.

2. Flat pry bar: Helps to remove old flashing and nails.

3. Hammer: Used for securing flashing with roofing nails.

4. Caulking gun and roofing sealant: Used to seal the edges of flashing and prevent water infiltration.

## Maintenance and Repair Tools:

Regular roof maintenance and timely repairs can extend the life of your roof. Keep these tools on hand for routine inspections and minor repairs:

1. Binoculars: Allow you to inspect your roof from the ground, identifying potential issues without climbing onto the roof.
2. Roof rake or leaf blower: Used to remove leaves, debris, and snow from your roof.
3. Caulking gun and roofing sealant: Used to seal around flashing and repair small leaks.
4. Patch kit: Contains self-adhesive patches and roofing cement for temporary repairs of small holes or cracks.

In addition to these essential tools, you may also need additional equipment depending on your specific roofing project and the materials you're working with. For example, if you're installing a metal roof, you may need a metal folding tool, a seaming tool, and a rivet gun.

Before starting any roofing project, ensure you have all the necessary tools and safety equipment on hand. Properly maintain your tools and store them in a secure, dry place to keep them in good condition for future use.

Remember, roofing work can be dangerous and requires a certain level of skill and knowledge. If you're unsure about your ability to complete a roofing project safely, don't hesitate to consult with or hire a professional roofing contractor. They have the expertise, experience, and specialized tools to get the job done right and ensure the longevity of your roof.

In the next section, we'll discuss the importance of roof inspection and maintenance, including how to identify signs of roof damage and perform routine maintenance tasks to keep your roof in top condition.

# Chapter 2
# Roof Inspection and Maintenance
## Identifying Signs of Roof Damage

Regular roof inspections and maintenance are essential for ensuring the longevity and performance of your roofing system. By identifying and addressing potential issues early on, you can prevent minor problems from turning into costly repairs or even premature roof failure. In this section, we'll discuss how to identify common signs of roof damage and what to look for during routine inspections.

**Interior Signs of Roof Damage:**
Before climbing onto your roof, start by inspecting your home's interior for signs of roof damage. Look for the following:
1. Water stains on ceilings or walls: If you notice discoloration, peeling paint, or sagging drywall, it could indicate a leak in your roof.
2. Light penetration in the attic: During the day, turn off the lights in your attic and look for any sunlight coming through the roof. This could signify holes or cracks in the roofing material.
3. Sagging roof deck: If your roof deck (the plywood or OSB layer beneath the shingles) appears to be sagging or feels spongy when walked on, it could be a sign of water damage or structural issues.
4. Increased energy bills: If your heating or cooling costs have suddenly spiked, it could be due to poor roof ventilation or insulation, which can lead to moisture buildup and damage.

**Exterior Signs of Roof Damage:**
Once you've checked your home's interior, it's time to inspect the exterior of your roof. Use binoculars to get a closer look, or if you feel comfortable and have the proper safety equipment, carefully climb onto the roof. Look for the following signs of damage:

1. Missing, cracked, or curling shingles: If you notice any shingles that are missing, cracked, curled, or blistered, it could indicate age-related wear or damage from severe weather.

2. Granule loss: As asphalt shingles age, they begin to lose the protective granules that help shield them from UV rays and the elements. If you notice excessive granules in your gutters or downspouts, it could be a sign that your shingles are nearing the end of their lifespan.

3. Rust or corrosion on metal components: If your roof has metal flashing, drip edges, or vents, check for signs of rust or corrosion. This could indicate a breakdown of the protective coating and lead to leaks.

4. Sagging or uneven roof planes: If your roof appears to be sagging or has uneven planes, it could signal structural damage or issues with the roof deck.

5. Moss, algae, or lichen growth: While not always a sign of damage, excessive growth of moss, algae, or lichen can trap moisture against your roof and lead to premature deterioration.

6. Damaged or clogged gutters: If your gutters are clogged with debris or pulling away from your home, they may not be able to properly channel water away from your roof and foundation.

7. Chimney or vent flashing issues: Check the flashing around your chimney, skylights, and vents for signs of damage, rust, or gaps. These areas are prone to leaks if not properly sealed.

**Seasonal Roof Inspections:**

In addition to checking for specific signs of damage, it's important to conduct thorough roof inspections at least twice a year – once in the spring and once in the fall. During these inspections, remove any debris from your roof and gutters, trim overhanging branches, and make note of any potential issues or areas that may require closer monitoring.

If you live in an area prone to severe weather events, such as hail storms, high winds, or heavy snowfall, it's a good idea to inspect your roof after each event to check for any damage that may have occurred.

**When to Call a Professional:**
If you identify any signs of significant damage or if you're unsure about the condition of your roof, it's always best to call in a professional roofing contractor. They have the knowledge, experience, and equipment to safely and thoroughly assess your roof and recommend the appropriate course of action.

Additionally, if your roof is nearing the end of its expected lifespan (which varies depending on the roofing material), it's a good idea to have a professional inspect it and provide an estimate for replacement.

By staying vigilant and addressing any potential issues early on, you can help extend the life of your roof and protect your home from water damage and other costly repairs. Remember, a well-maintained roof not only enhances your home's curb appeal but also plays a crucial role in safeguarding your family and belongings.

In the next section, we'll discuss the importance of regular roof maintenance and outline some key tasks you can perform to keep your roof in top shape year-round.

# Conducting a Thorough Roof Inspection

A comprehensive roof inspection is essential for identifying potential issues and ensuring your roof is in good condition. By following a systematic approach and knowing what to look for, you can catch problems early and extend the life of your roofing system. In this section, we'll walk through the steps of conducting a thorough roof inspection.

## Step 1: Prepare for the Inspection
Before starting your inspection, gather the necessary tools and safety equipment:
- Binoculars
- Camera or smartphone for documentation
- Flashlight
- Ladder (if accessing the roof)
- Safety gear (non-slip shoes, gloves, hard hat, and fall protection harness if needed)
- Notepad and pen for taking notes

## Step 2: Inspect the Interior
Begin your inspection inside your home, focusing on the attic and ceilings. Look for:
1. Water stains, discoloration, or sagging on ceilings and walls
2. Signs of moisture, mold, or mildew in the attic
3. Proper insulation and ventilation in the attic
4. Daylight penetrating through the roof deck

## Step 3: Examine the Exterior Roof Surface
Next, use binoculars to visually inspect the exterior roof surface from the ground. If safe and accessible, you can also use a ladder to get a closer look. Check for:
1. Missing, cracked, curled, or blistered shingles
2. Uneven or sagging roof planes
3. Granule loss on asphalt shingles

4. Rust or corrosion on metal components
5. Moss, algae, or lichen growth
6. Damaged or missing flashing around chimneys, vents, and skylights

**Step 4: Check the Gutters and Downspouts**
Properly functioning gutters and downspouts are crucial for directing water away from your roof and foundation. Inspect them for:
1. Clogs or debris buildup
2. Cracks, holes, or rust
3. Sagging or pulling away from the roof
4. Downspouts directing water at least 5 feet away from the foundation

**Step 5: Assess the Roof Penetrations**
Roof penetrations, such as chimneys, vents, and skylights, are common areas for leaks. Examine them closely for:
1. Damaged, missing, or improperly sealed flashing
2. Cracks or gaps in the sealant
3. Rust or corrosion on metal components
4. Damaged or missing shingles around the penetrations

Step 6: Inspect the Roof Edges and Overhangs
The edges and overhangs of your roof are exposed to the elements and can be prone to damage. Check for:
1. Damaged or missing drip edges
2. Sagging or rotting fascia boards
3. Peeling or blistering paint on soffits
4. Animal or insect nests or damage

## Step 7: Document Your Findings

As you conduct your inspection, take detailed notes and photographs of any issues you discover. This documentation will be helpful when communicating with a professional roofing contractor or when filing an insurance claim if needed.

## Step 8: Determine the Next Steps

Based on your inspection findings, decide on the necessary course of action:

1. If you identified minor issues, such as clogged gutters or small amounts of debris, address these problems yourself.
2. If you discovered more significant issues or are unsure about the severity of a problem, contact a professional roofing contractor for a more detailed assessment and recommendation.
3. If your roof is nearing the end of its expected lifespan or has extensive damage, consider scheduling a roof replacement.

Remember, safety should always be your top priority when conducting a roof inspection. If you are uncomfortable with heights, lack the necessary safety equipment, or encounter a potentially dangerous situation, do not hesitate to contact a professional roofing contractor to perform the inspection for you.

Regular roof inspections, at least twice a year and after severe weather events, are crucial for maintaining the integrity and longevity of your roofing system. By identifying and addressing issues promptly, you can prevent minor problems from escalating into costly repairs or premature roof failure.

In the next section, we'll discuss the importance of regular roof maintenance and provide a checklist of tasks you can perform to keep your roof in optimal condition year-round.

# Regular Maintenance Tasks to Extend Your Roof's Lifespan

Performing regular maintenance on your roof is crucial for extending its lifespan and preventing costly repairs. By implementing a consistent roof maintenance routine, you can identify and address potential issues before they escalate, ensuring your roof continues to protect your home for years to come. In this section, we'll outline the key maintenance tasks you should perform to keep your roof in top condition.

## 1. Clean Gutters and Downspouts

Clogged gutters and downspouts can cause water to overflow and seep under your roofing material, leading to leaks and water damage. To prevent this, clean your gutters and downspouts at least twice a year, or more frequently if you have many trees near your home.

- Remove leaves, twigs, and other debris from gutters and downspouts
- Check for any cracks, holes, or rust, and repair or replace damaged sections as needed
- Ensure downspouts direct water at least 5 feet away from your foundation

## 2. Trim Overhanging Branches

Overhanging tree branches can scratch or puncture your roofing material, leading to damage and potential leaks. They also provide access for pests and contribute to debris buildup on your roof.

- Trim any branches that are touching or hanging close to your roof
- Ensure there is at least a 10-foot clearance between your roof and tree branches
- Consider removing any trees that pose a significant threat to your roof

### 3. Remove Debris from the Roof

Accumulation of debris, such as leaves, twigs, and moss, can trap moisture against your roof and lead to premature deterioration. Regularly remove debris from your roof to prevent damage and extend its lifespan.

- Use a roof rake or leaf blower to gently remove debris from your roof
- Pay extra attention to valleys and areas around roof penetrations where debris tends to accumulate
- Avoid using a pressure washer, as it can damage your roofing material

### 4. Inspect and Repair Flashing

Flashing is the metal material used to seal and waterproof areas around chimneys, vents, skylights, and other roof penetrations. Over time, flashing can become damaged or loose, allowing water to seep into your home.

- Inspect flashing for signs of rust, corrosion, or damage
- Ensure flashing is properly sealed and secured to your roof and the adjoining structure
- Apply a fresh bead of roofing cement or sealant around the edges of the flashing if needed

### 5. Check for Loose, Damaged, or Missing Shingles

Regularly inspect your roof for any signs of shingle damage, such as loose, cracked, curled, or missing shingles. Promptly replace damaged shingles to prevent leaks and further deterioration.

- Check for shingles that have become loose or dislodged due to wind or impact
- Replace any cracked, curled, or missing shingles with new ones that match your existing roofing material
- Secure loose shingles with roofing cement or nails as needed

## 6. Maintain Proper Ventilation

Proper roof ventilation helps regulate temperature and moisture levels in your attic, preventing issues like heat buildup, ice dams, and mold growth. Ensure your roof has adequate ventilation and keep vents clear of obstruction.

- Check that your roof has a balanced system of intake vents (soffit or eave vents) and exhaust vents (ridge or gable vents)
- Ensure attic insulation does not block the flow of air through the vents
- Remove any debris or obstructions from vent openings

## 7. Inspect and Repair Roof Sealant

Roof sealant, also known as caulking, is used to seal around flashing, roof penetrations, and other areas prone to leaks. Over time, sealant can crack, peel, or degrade, allowing water to penetrate your roof.

- Inspect sealant around flashing, vents, and other penetrations for signs of cracking, peeling, or gaps
- Remove old, damaged sealant and replace it with a fresh bead of high-quality roofing sealant
- Smooth the sealant to ensure proper adhesion and coverage

## 8. Schedule Professional Inspections

While regular self-inspections and maintenance are essential, it's also important to schedule professional roof inspections every few years or after severe weather events. A professional roofing contractor can identify issues that may not be visible to the untrained eye and provide expert advice on repairs and maintenance.

- Schedule a professional inspection every 2-3 years, or more frequently if recommended by your roofing contractor
- Have your roof inspected after severe storms, hail, or high winds to check for damage

- Keep records of professional inspections and repairs for future reference and warranty purposes

By incorporating these regular maintenance tasks into your home maintenance routine, you can prolong the life of your roof and avoid costly repairs. Remember to always prioritize safety when performing any roof maintenance, and don't hesitate to call in a professional if you encounter a task that is beyond your skill level or comfort zone.

Regular roof maintenance, combined with prompt repairs and professional inspections, will help ensure your roof remains a reliable, protective barrier for your home and family for many years to come. In the next chapter, we'll dive into the specifics of shingle installation and replacement, providing step-by-step guidance for tackling this common roofing project.

# Chapter 3
# Shingle Installation and Replacement
## Preparing Your Roof for Shingle Installation

Proper preparation is key to ensuring a successful and long-lasting shingle installation. Whether you're installing shingles on a new roof or replacing old, worn-out shingles, taking the time to correctly prepare your roof will help prevent future issues and extend the life of your roofing system. In this section, we'll walk through the essential steps for preparing your roof for shingle installation.

### Step 1: Assess the Roof Deck
The roof deck, also known as sheathing, is the plywood or oriented strand board (OSB) layer that serves as the foundation for your roofing material. Before installing new shingles, it's crucial to ensure that the roof deck is in good condition.

- Inspect the roof deck for any signs of water damage, rot, or sagging
- Check for loose, missing, or protruding nails, and either replace or hammer them flush
- Replace any damaged or rotted sections of the roof deck with new plywood or OSB
- Ensure the roof deck is properly attached to the rafters or trusses, and add nails or screws as needed

### Step 2: Remove Old Roofing Material
If you're replacing old shingles, you'll need to remove the existing roofing material down to the roof deck. This process is known as a tear-off.

- Start at the highest point of the roof and work your way down
- Use a roofing tear-off shovel or spade to remove the old shingles and nails

- Remove any remaining nails with a pry bar or hammer
- Dispose of the old roofing material properly, as it may contain asbestos or other hazardous materials

## Step 3: Repair or Replace Flashing

Flashing is the metal material used to seal and waterproof areas around chimneys, vents, skylights, and other roof penetrations. Before installing new shingles, repair or replace any damaged or worn flashing.

- Remove old flashing and clean the surrounding area
- Inspect the roof deck and framing around the penetration for any signs of water damage or rot, and repair as needed
- Install new flashing according to the manufacturer's instructions, ensuring it is properly sealed and secured to the roof deck

## Step 4: Install Drip Edge

Drip edge is an L-shaped metal strip that is installed along the edges of the roof to help guide water away from the fascia and into the gutters. It also provides a clean, finished look to the roof edges.

- Install drip edge along the eaves, ensuring it extends over the gutter
- Secure the drip edge to the roof deck with roofing nails, spacing them about 12 inches apart
- Overlap the drip edge pieces by about 2 inches at the joints

## Step 5: Apply Underlayment

Underlayment is a protective barrier that is installed over the roof deck before the shingles are applied. It helps protect the roof deck from water infiltration and provides an additional layer of insulation.

- Start at the bottom edge of the roof and work your way up, overlapping each row by about 4 inches

- Use roofing nails or staples to secure the underlayment to the roof deck
- Apply a layer of self-adhering ice and water shield along the eaves and in valleys, as these areas are prone to water infiltration

## Step 6: Mark the Shingle Layout

Before installing the shingles, it's important to plan and mark the layout to ensure a straight, even appearance.

- Use a chalk line to snap horizontal lines across the roof, starting at the bottom edge and working your way up
- Space the lines according to the exposure of the shingles (the portion of each shingle that will be visible when installed)
- Adjust the layout as needed to ensure the shingles will align properly with the roof edges and penetrations

## Step 7: Prepare the Shingles

Before installing the shingles, it's important to properly prepare them to ensure optimal performance and appearance.

- Store the shingles in a cool, dry place until ready to use
- Separate any shingles that are stuck together, as they may tear or deform during installation
- For laminated or architectural shingles, ensure the adhesive strips are facing up and oriented toward the peak of the roof

By properly preparing your roof for shingle installation, you'll create a solid foundation for a durable, long-lasting roofing system. Taking the time to assess and repair the roof deck, install proper flashing and underlayment, and plan the shingle layout will help ensure a successful installation and prevent future issues.

Remember to always prioritize safety when working on your roof. Wear appropriate footwear, use proper fall protection equipment, and avoid working in wet or windy conditions. If you're unsure about any step of the process or encounter a situation beyond your skill level, don't hesitate to consult with a professional roofing contractor.

In the next section, we'll provide a step-by-step guide for installing asphalt shingles, including tips and best practices for achieving a professional-looking result.

# Step-by-Step Guide to Installing Asphalt Shingles

Installing asphalt shingles is a straightforward process that can be accomplished by most DIY enthusiasts with the right tools and preparation. By following this step-by-step guide, you can ensure a proper installation that will protect your home from the elements for years to come.

### Step 1: Install the Starter Strip

The starter strip is a row of shingles that is installed along the eaves of the roof to provide a seal and prevent water infiltration.

- Cut the tabs off a row of shingles to create the starter strip
- Align the starter strip with the drip edge, ensuring it overhangs the eaves by about 1/4 to 3/8 inch
- Secure the starter strip to the roof deck with roofing nails, placing them about 2 to 3 inches from the eave edge and spacing them 12 to 16 inches apart

### Step 2: Install the First Course

The first course of shingles sets the foundation for the rest of the installation and ensures a straight, even appearance.

- Start at the bottom left corner of the roof, aligning the first shingle with the starter strip and the drip edge
- Secure the shingle to the roof deck with roofing nails, placing them just below the sealant strip and about 1 inch from each edge
- Continue installing shingles along the first course, butting each shingle up against the previous one without overlapping
- Use a utility knife to trim the last shingle in the course to fit the remaining space

## Step 3: Install Subsequent Courses

With the first course in place, you can begin installing the subsequent courses of shingles, working your way up the roof.

- Start the second course by cutting a shingle in half and aligning it with the left edge of the roof, ensuring it overlaps the first course by about half the length of the shingle
- Secure the shingle to the roof deck with roofing nails, placing them just below the sealant strip and about 1 inch from each edge
- Continue installing shingles along the second course, butting each shingle up against the previous one without overlapping
- Repeat this process for each subsequent course, offsetting the shingles by half the width of a shingle to create a staggered pattern

## Step 4: Install Shingles Around Roof Penetrations

When you encounter a roof penetration, such as a vent or chimney, you'll need to carefully cut and install the shingles to ensure a proper seal.

- Install shingles up to the bottom edge of the penetration, trimming them as needed to fit
- Cut a shingle to fit around the sides of the penetration, ensuring it extends past the penetration by at least 4 inches
- Apply a bead of roofing cement around the penetration and slide the cut shingle underneath, pressing it firmly into the cement
- Install shingles above the penetration, trimming them as needed to fit and ensuring they overlap the flashing by at least 4 inches

## Step 5: Install Ridge Cap Shingles

Ridge cap shingles are installed along the peak of the roof to provide a finished look and protect against water infiltration.

Cut a ridge cap shingle into three equal pieces, and fold each piece over the peak of the roof

- Secure each piece to the roof deck with roofing nails, placing them about 1 inch from each edge and ensuring they penetrate both sides of the roof
- Continue installing ridge cap shingles along the peak, overlapping each piece by about 6 inches and ensuring a tight, secure fit

## Step 6: Seal and Clean Up

Once all the shingles are installed, it's important to seal any exposed nails and clean up the work area.

- Apply a small dab of roofing cement over each exposed roofing nail to prevent leaks
- Remove any loose debris or shingle scraps from the roof and gutters
- Dispose of any waste materials properly, and store any leftover shingles in a cool, dry place for future repairs

By following these steps and taking the time to properly install your asphalt shingles, you can ensure a durable, long-lasting roofing system that will protect your home from the elements. Remember to always prioritize safety when working on your roof, and don't hesitate to consult with a professional roofing contractor if you encounter any issues or have concerns about the installation process.

Regular maintenance, such as cleaning gutters, trimming overhanging branches, and inspecting for signs of damage, will help extend the life of your new shingle roof and prevent future issues. With proper installation and care, your asphalt shingle roof can provide reliable protection for your home for 20 to 30 years or more.

In the next section, we'll discuss how to replace damaged or missing shingles, including tips for identifying and addressing common issues that may arise over the life of your roof.

# Replacing Damaged or Missing Shingles

Even with proper installation and regular maintenance, your asphalt shingle roof may experience damage or shingle loss over time due to severe weather, impact, or age-related wear and tear. Promptly replacing damaged or missing shingles is essential to maintaining the integrity of your roofing system and preventing leaks and further deterioration. In this section, we'll provide a detailed guide on how to identify and replace damaged or missing shingles.

## Identifying Damaged or Missing Shingles

Before you can replace damaged or missing shingles, you need to locate and assess the affected areas of your roof. Here are some common signs to look for:

- Missing shingles: Look for gaps or exposed areas on your roof where shingles have completely fallen off or blown away.
- Cracked or broken shingles: Inspect your roof for shingles that have cracks, splits, or breaks, as these can allow water to penetrate the underlayment and cause leaks.
- Curled or lifted shingles: Look for shingles that have curled edges or are lifting up from the roof deck, as these can be signs of age-related wear or improper installation.
- Granule loss: Check your gutters and downspouts for excessive granule buildup, as this can indicate that your shingles are losing their protective coating and nearing the end of their lifespan.

## Tools and Materials Needed

Before you begin replacing damaged or missing shingles, gather the following tools and materials:

- Replacement shingles (matching the color and style of your existing roof)
- Roofing nails
- Hammer

- Pry bar
- Utility knife
- Roofing cement
- Caulking gun
- Safety gear (ladder, non-slip shoes, work gloves, and fall protection harness if needed)

## Replacing a Damaged Shingle

To replace a damaged shingle, follow these steps:

1. Carefully lift the edges of the shingle above the damaged one, and use a pry bar to remove the nails securing the damaged shingle to the roof deck.

2. Slide the damaged shingle out from under the row above it, being careful not to tear or damage the surrounding shingles.

3. Use a utility knife to scrape away any remaining roofing cement or debris from the roof deck where the damaged shingle was located.

4. Take a new shingle and trim it to fit the space left by the removed shingle, if necessary.

5. Slide the new shingle into place, ensuring it aligns properly with the surrounding shingles and overlaps the shingle below it by about half the length of the shingle.

6. Secure the new shingle to the roof deck using roofing nails, placing them just below the sealant strip and about 1 inch from each edge.

7. Apply a small dab of roofing cement over each nail head to prevent leaks, and press the shingles above the replacement shingle back into place.

## Replacing a Missing Shingle

To replace a missing shingle, follow these steps:

- 1. Locate the area where the shingle is missing, and use a pry bar to carefully lift the edges of the shingles above and on either side of the gap.

2. Use a utility knife to scrape away any remaining roofing cement or debris from the roof deck in the gap.

3. Take a new shingle and trim it to fit the space left by the missing shingle, if necessary.

4. Slide the new shingle into place, ensuring it aligns properly with the surrounding shingles and overlaps the shingle below it by about half the length of the shingle.

5. Secure the new shingle to the roof deck using roofing nails, placing them just below the sealant strip and about 1 inch from each edge.

6. Apply a small dab of roofing cement over each nail head to prevent leaks, and press the surrounding shingles back into place.

Tips for Successful Shingle Replacement
- Always prioritize safety when working on your roof, and use proper fall protection equipment if necessary.
- Work on a cool, dry day to prevent the shingles from becoming too pliable or brittle.
- If you're unsure about any step of the process or encounter a situation beyond your skill level, don't hesitate to consult with a professional roofing contractor.
- Regularly inspect your roof for signs of damage or wear, and address any issues promptly to prevent further deterioration.

By promptly replacing damaged or missing shingles and following these guidelines, you can help extend the life of your asphalt shingle roof and ensure it continues to protect your home from the elements. Remember, if you encounter widespread damage or are unsure about the condition of your roof, it's always best to consult with a professional roofing contractor for an assessment and recommendation.

In the next section, we'll discuss the importance of flashing installation and repair, including how to properly install and maintain flashing around chimneys, vents, and other roof penetrations to prevent leaks and water damage.

# Chapter 4
# Flashing Installation and Repair
## The Purpose of Flashing and Common Installation Areas

Flashing is a crucial component of any roofing system, as it helps to seal and waterproof vulnerable areas where the roof meets walls, chimneys, vents, or other protrusions. Properly installed and maintained flashing is essential for preventing leaks, water damage, and premature deterioration of your roof. In this section, we'll discuss the purpose of flashing and the most common areas where it is installed.

### The Purpose of Flashing

Flashing serves several important functions in a roofing system:

1. Waterproofing: The primary purpose of flashing is to prevent water from penetrating the roof at joints, edges, and penetrations. By directing water away from these vulnerable areas, flashing helps to maintain the integrity of the roof and protect the interior of the building from leaks and water damage.

2. Sealing: Flashing helps to seal gaps and cracks between the roofing material and adjacent surfaces, such as walls or chimneys. This prevents air and moisture infiltration, which can lead to issues like energy loss, condensation, and mold growth.

3. Reinforcement: Flashing provides additional reinforcement to areas of the roof that are subject to high stress or movement, such as valleys or roof-to-wall intersections. This helps to prevent cracking, splitting, or tearing of the roofing material in these high-stress areas.

4. Aesthetics: In addition to its functional benefits, flashing also contributes to the overall appearance of the roof. Properly installed and maintained flashing creates a clean, finished look and can enhance the visual appeal of the building.

## Common Flashing Installation Areas

Flashing is typically installed in the following areas of a roof:

1. Chimneys: Flashing is installed around the base of chimneys to prevent water from seeping into the gap between the chimney and the roof. This type of flashing is usually made of two parts: step flashing, which is installed under the shingles and bent to fit the contour of the chimney, and counterflashing, which is embedded in the mortar joints of the chimney and overlaps the step flashing.

2. Vents and Pipes: Flashing is installed around plumbing vents, exhaust vents, and other pipes that penetrate the roof. This type of flashing is typically a pre-formed rubber or plastic boot that fits snugly around the pipe and is sealed to the roof with roofing cement or sealant.

3. Skylights: Flashing is installed around the perimeter of skylights to prevent water from seeping into the gap between the skylight and the roof. This type of flashing is usually made of metal and is custom-fitted to the size and shape of the skylight.

4. Valleys: Flashing is installed in the valleys of the roof, where two sloping roof planes meet. Valley flashing helps to channel water down the valley and off the roof, preventing it from seeping under the shingles and causing leaks.

5. Roof-to-Wall Intersections: Flashing is installed where the roof meets a vertical wall, such as a dormer or a second-story exterior wall. This type of flashing, called step flashing, is installed under the siding or wall cladding and over the roofing material to create a waterproof seal.

6. Drip Edges: Flashing is installed along the edges of the roof, either at the eaves or the rakes (gable ends). Drip edge flashing helps to guide water away from the fascia and into the gutters, preventing it from seeping under the roofing material and causing damage to the roof deck or fascia.

Proper flashing installation is critical for the long-term performance and durability of your roofing system. When installing or replacing flashing, it's important to use high-quality materials that are compatible with your roofing material and to follow the manufacturer's instructions and industry best practices for installation.

In the next section, we'll provide a step-by-step guide for installing flashing around chimneys, vents, and skylights, including tips for achieving a proper seal and ensuring long-lasting protection against leaks and water damage.

# Installing Flashing Around Chimneys, Vents, and Skylights

Properly installing flashing around chimneys, vents, and skylights is crucial for preventing leaks and water damage in these vulnerable areas of your roof. In this section, we'll provide a detailed, step-by-step guide for installing flashing around these common roof penetrations, along with tips for achieving a durable, long-lasting seal.

### Installing Flashing Around Chimneys

Step 1: Prepare the area
- Remove any existing flashing and clean the area around the chimney, ensuring the surface is free of debris and loose mortar.
- Cut a groove into the mortar joint of the chimney, about 1 to 1 1/2 inches deep, to accommodate the counterflashing.

Step 2: Install the base flashing
- Cut a piece of base flashing (also called step flashing) to fit the width of the chimney and extend up the chimney by at least 4 inches.
- Bend the base flashing to a 90-degree angle to fit the corner of the chimney and the roof.
- Secure the base flashing to the roof deck with roofing nails, and seal the nail heads with roofing cement.

Step 3: Install the step flashing
- Cut pieces of step flashing to fit the width of the shingles and extend up the chimney by at least 4 inches.
- Install the step flashing under each shingle course, bending it to fit the contour of the chimney and overlapping each piece by at least 2 inches.

- Secure the step flashing to the roof deck with roofing nails, and seal the nail heads with roofing cement.

Step 4: Install the counterflashing
- Cut a piece of counterflashing to fit the width of the chimney and extend down over the step flashing by at least 4 inches.
- Insert the counterflashing into the groove cut in the mortar joint, and secure it in place with masonry anchors or screws.
- Seal the top of the counterflashing with a bead of silicone caulk or roofing cement.

## Installing Flashing Around Vents and Pipes

Step 1: Choose the right flashing
- Select a pre-formed rubber or plastic vent boot that is compatible with your roofing material and fits snugly around the vent or pipe.
- Ensure the flashing has a wide flange at the base to provide adequate coverage and sealing on the roof surface.

Step 2: Prepare the vent or pipe
- Clean the area around the vent or pipe, removing any debris or old flashing material.
- Apply a bead of silicone caulk or roofing cement around the base of the vent or pipe to create a seal.

Step 3: Install the flashing
- Slide the vent boot over the vent or pipe, ensuring it fits snugly and the base flange sits flat on the roof surface.
- Secure the base flange to the roof deck with roofing nails, spacing them evenly around the perimeter.
- Seal the nail heads and the edge of the base flange with a bead of roofing cement or silicone caulk.

Step 4: Integrate with shingles
- Install shingles around the vent boot, overlapping the base flange by at least 2 inches on all sides.
- Trim the shingles as needed to fit snugly around the vent boot, and seal any exposed edges with roofing cement.

## Installing Flashing Around Skylights

Step 1: Prepare the skylight and roof deck
- Clean the area around the skylight, removing any debris or old flashing material.
- Apply a bead of silicone caulk or roofing cement around the perimeter of the skylight to create a seal.
- Install a layer of self-adhering underlayment around the skylight, extending it up the sides of the curb and onto the roof deck by at least 6 inches.

Step 2: Install the base flashing
- Cut pieces of base flashing to fit the width of the skylight and extend onto the roof deck by at least 4 inches.
- Bend the base flashing to fit the contour of the skylight curb, and secure it to the roof deck with roofing nails.
- Seal the nail heads and the edges of the base flashing with roofing cement or silicone caulk.

Step 3: Install the counterflashing
- Cut pieces of counterflashing to fit the width of the skylight and extend down over the base flashing by at least 4 inches.
- Secure the counterflashing to the skylight curb with screws or rivets, spacing them evenly around the perimeter.
- Seal the top of the counterflashing with a bead of silicone caulk or roofing cement.

Step 4: Integrate with shingles
- Install shingles around the skylight, overlapping the base flashing and counterflashing by at least 2 inches on all sides.
- Trim the shingles as needed to fit snugly around the skylight, and seal any exposed edges with roofing cement.

Tips for Successful Flashing Installation
- Always use high-quality, durable flashing materials that are compatible with your roofing system.
- Ensure that all flashing pieces are properly lapped and sealed to prevent water infiltration.
- Use a generous amount of roofing cement or silicone caulk to seal all edges, seams, and nail heads.
- Regularly inspect and maintain your flashing to ensure it remains in good condition and provides lasting protection against leaks and water damage.

By following these step-by-step guidelines and tips for installing flashing around chimneys, vents, and skylights, you can help ensure the long-term performance and durability of your roofing system. If you are unsure about any step of the process or encounter a situation beyond your skill level, don't hesitate to consult with a professional roofing contractor for assistance.

In the next section, we'll discuss how to identify and repair damaged or leaking flashing, including common signs of flashing failure and the steps involved in making effective repairs.

# Repairing Damaged or Leaking Flashing

Even with proper installation, flashing can become damaged or deteriorate over time due to exposure to the elements, physical impact, or age-related wear and tear. Promptly identifying and repairing damaged or leaking flashing is essential for preventing water infiltration and maintaining the integrity of your roofing system. In this section, we'll discuss how to identify common signs of flashing failure and provide a detailed guide for repairing damaged or leaking flashing.

### Identifying Damaged or Leaking Flashing

Regularly inspecting your roof and flashing can help you identify potential issues before they lead to serious damage. Look for the following signs of flashing failure:

1. Water stains or dampness on interior walls or ceilings near roof penetrations, such as chimneys, vents, or skylights.
2. Visible cracks, gaps, or holes in the flashing material.
3. Rust or corrosion on metal flashing, which can indicate a breakdown of the protective coating.
4. Loose or missing fasteners, such as nails or screws, that secure the flashing to the roof or adjacent structures.
5. Sagging or pulled-away flashing that no longer sits flush against the roof surface or penetration.
6. Deteriorated or crumbling sealant around the edges of the flashing.

If you notice any of these signs, it's important to address the issue promptly to prevent further damage and water infiltration.

## Repairing Damaged or Leaking Flashing

Step 1: Safety first
- Before beginning any repairs, ensure that you have proper safety equipment, such as non-slip shoes, gloves, and a secured ladder.
- If the roof is steep or you are uncomfortable working at heights, consider hiring a professional roofing contractor to perform the repairs.

Step 2: Clean the area
- Remove any debris, dirt, or loose material from the area around the damaged flashing.
- Use a wire brush or scraper to remove any old sealant, rust, or corrosion from the flashing surface.

Step 3: Assess the damage
- Determine the extent of the damage and whether the flashing can be repaired or if it needs to be replaced entirely.
- For minor cracks or holes, the flashing may be repairable using a compatible sealant or patching material.
- If the flashing is extensively damaged, corroded, or pulled away from the roof surface, it may need to be replaced.

Step 4: Repair minor damage
- For small cracks or holes, apply a generous bead of roofing cement or silicone caulk to the damaged area, smoothing it with a putty knife to create a watertight seal.
- If the flashing is loose or pulled away from the roof surface, use a flat pry bar to carefully lift the surrounding shingles and reposition the flashing.
- Secure the flashing with new roofing nails or screws, and seal the fastener heads with roofing cement.

Step 5: Replace severely damaged flashing
- If the flashing is beyond repair, carefully remove the damaged section without disturbing the surrounding roofing material.
- Measure and cut a new piece of flashing to fit the area, ensuring it overlaps the existing flashing by at least 4 inches on all sides.
- Secure the new flashing with roofing nails or screws, and seal the fastener heads and edges with roofing cement.
- Reposition any displaced shingles and seal them with roofing cement to ensure a watertight connection.

Step 6: Apply sealant and perform final inspection
- Apply a bead of roofing cement or silicone caulk around the perimeter of the repaired or replaced flashing to create a watertight seal.
- Inspect the entire area to ensure that the flashing is properly secured, sealed, and integrated with the surrounding roofing material.
- Check for any remaining signs of damage or potential leaks, and address them as needed.

Tips for Maintaining Flashing
- Regularly inspect your roof and flashing for signs of damage or deterioration, especially after severe weather events.
- Keep your roof and gutters clean and free of debris to prevent damage to the flashing and other roofing components.
- When making repairs, always use high-quality, compatible materials and follow the manufacturer's instructions for application and curing times.
- If you are unsure about the extent of the damage or the proper repair method, consult with a professional roofing contractor to ensure the issue is addressed correctly.

By promptly identifying and repairing damaged or leaking flashing, you can help extend the life of your roofing system and protect your home from costly water damage. Remember to prioritize safety and consult with a professional if you are unsure about any aspect of the repair process.

In the next section, we'll explore the importance of proper roof ventilation and discuss the various types of ventilation systems available for maintaining a healthy, energy-efficient roofing system.

# Chapter 5
# Ventilation System Installation and Maintenance

## The Importance of Proper Roof Ventilation

Proper roof ventilation is a critical component of a healthy, long-lasting roofing system. A well-designed ventilation system helps to regulate temperature and moisture levels in your attic space, which can prevent a wide range of issues that can compromise the integrity and energy efficiency of your home. In this section, we'll discuss the importance of proper roof ventilation and explain how it contributes to the overall performance of your roofing system.

### Benefits of Proper Roof Ventilation

1. Temperature regulation
- Adequate ventilation helps to prevent heat buildup in your attic during the summer months, which can make your home more comfortable and reduce the workload on your air conditioning system.
- In the winter, proper ventilation helps to maintain a consistent temperature between the attic and the living space, preventing the formation of ice dams and other cold-weather issues.

2. Moisture control
- Excess moisture in your attic can lead to a range of problems, including mold growth, wood rot, and damage to insulation and structural components.
- Proper ventilation allows moisture to escape from the attic, helping to prevent condensation and maintain a healthy, dry environment.

3. Energy efficiency
- By regulating temperature and moisture levels, a well-ventilated attic can help to reduce energy costs associated with heating and cooling your home.
- Adequate ventilation can also help to extend the life of your roofing materials by preventing premature aging and deterioration caused by heat and moisture buildup.

4. Improved air quality
- A properly ventilated attic can help to prevent the buildup of pollutants, allergens, and other harmful substances that can compromise indoor air quality.
- By allowing fresh air to circulate through the attic space, ventilation can help to create a healthier living environment for you and your family.

5. Compliance with building codes
- Most local building codes require a minimum level of roof ventilation to ensure the safety, durability, and energy efficiency of residential structures.
- By installing and maintaining a proper ventilation system, you can help to ensure that your home meets these important standards and regulations.

**How Roof Ventilation Works**

A typical roof ventilation system consists of two main components: intake vents and exhaust vents. These vents work together to create a continuous flow of air through the attic space, helping to regulate temperature and moisture levels.

1. Intake vents
- Intake vents are typically located along the lower edge of the roof, in the soffit or eave area.

- These vents allow cool, fresh air to enter the attic space, providing a source of ventilation and helping to replace the warm, moist air that tends to accumulate in the attic.

2. Exhaust vents
- Exhaust vents are located near the peak of the roof, either on the ridgeline or in the gable ends.
- These vents allow warm, moist air to escape from the attic, helping to create a continuous flow of air and prevent the buildup of heat and humidity.

The specific type and placement of intake and exhaust vents will depend on factors such as the size and configuration of your roof, the local climate conditions, and the requirements of your building code.

**Maintaining Proper Roof Ventilation**
To ensure that your roof ventilation system continues to function effectively over time, it's important to perform regular maintenance and inspections. Some key steps for maintaining proper roof ventilation include:

1. Keep vents clear of obstructions
- Regularly check your intake and exhaust vents to ensure that they are free of debris, such as leaves, twigs, and animal nests.
- Use a brush or vacuum to remove any blockages that could impede the flow of air through the vents.

2. Inspect vents for damage
- Check your vents for signs of physical damage, such as cracks, gaps, or missing components.
- Repair or replace any damaged vents promptly to maintain the integrity of your ventilation system.

3. Ensure adequate insulation
- Proper insulation is essential for maintaining the effectiveness of your roof ventilation system.
- Ensure that your attic has the recommended level of insulation for your climate zone, and that the insulation is installed correctly to allow for proper airflow.

4. Monitor indoor humidity levels
- Use a hygrometer to monitor the humidity levels in your home, particularly in the attic space.
- If you notice persistently high humidity levels, it may be a sign that your ventilation system is not functioning correctly and needs to be evaluated by a professional.

5. Schedule regular professional inspections
- Have your roof ventilation system inspected by a qualified roofing contractor at least once a year, or more frequently if you live in an area with severe weather conditions.
- A professional inspection can help to identify potential issues early on and ensure that your ventilation system is functioning optimally.

By understanding the importance of proper roof ventilation and taking steps to maintain your ventilation system over time, you can help to protect the integrity of your roofing system, improve the energy efficiency of your home, and create a healthier, more comfortable living environment for you and your family.

In the next section, we'll take a closer look at the different types of roof vents available, including ridge vents, soffit vents, and gable vents, and discuss the key factors to consider when selecting and installing a ventilation system for your home.

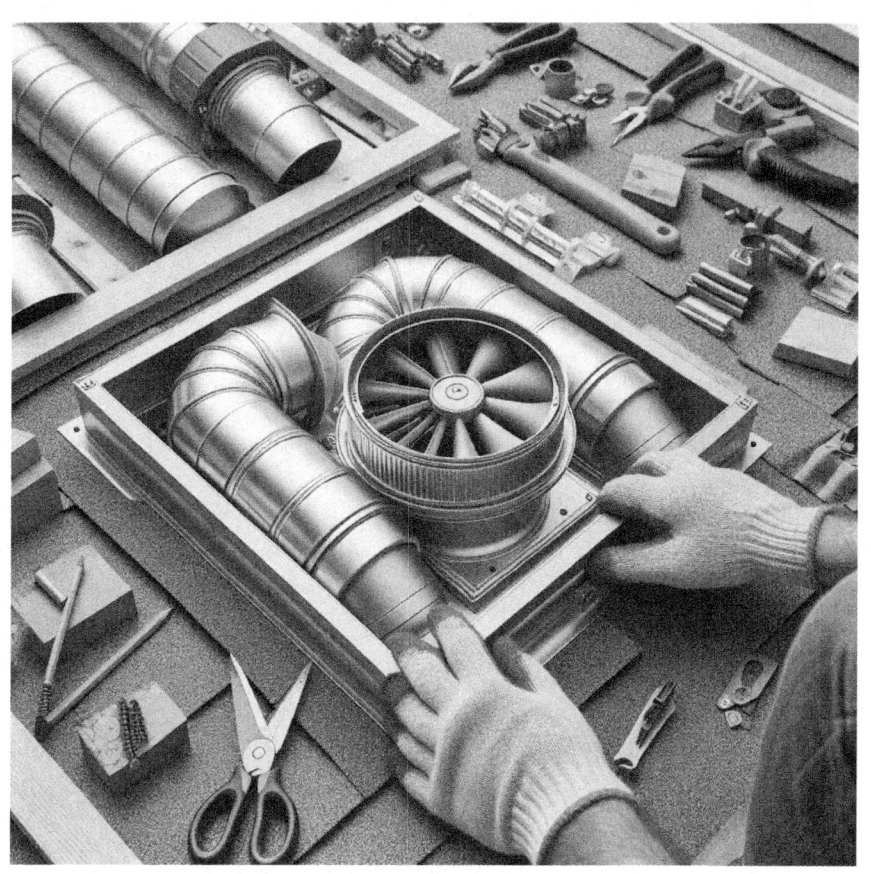

# Types of Roof Vents: Ridge, Soffit, and Gable Vents

When it comes to designing an effective roof ventilation system, there are several types of vents available, each with its own unique benefits and installation requirements. In this section, we'll explore three of the most common types of roof vents: ridge vents, soffit vents, and gable vents. We'll discuss the key features and advantages of each type, and provide guidance on how to select and install the right vents for your home.

### 1. Ridge Vents

Ridge vents are installed along the peak of the roof, where they allow warm, moist air to escape from the attic space. They are one of the most popular and effective types of exhaust vents, thanks to their ability to provide continuous, uniform ventilation along the entire length of the roof.

Advantages of ridge vents:
- Provide a clean, streamlined appearance that blends in with the roofline
- Allow for even distribution of ventilation across the attic space
- Work well in conjunction with soffit vents to create a balanced ventilation system
- Help to prevent the formation of ice dams and other cold-weather issues

Installation considerations:
- Ridge vents should be installed along the entire length of the roof peak, with a gap of at least 1 inch between the vent and the roof decking to allow for proper airflow
- The size and capacity of the ridge vent should be matched to the size and ventilation requirements of the attic space
- Ridge vents should be installed in conjunction with soffit vents to create a balanced ventilation system

## 2. Soffit Vents

Soffit vents are installed in the underside of the eaves, where they allow cool, fresh air to enter the attic space. They work in conjunction with ridge vents or other exhaust vents to create a continuous flow of air through the attic.

Advantages of soffit vents:
- Provide a source of intake ventilation that helps to balance the exhaust ventilation provided by ridge vents or other types of vents
- Help to prevent moisture buildup and condensation in the attic space
- Can be installed in a variety of styles and configurations to suit the specific needs of your home

Installation considerations:
- Soffit vents should be installed in a continuous strip along the entire length of the eaves, with a minimum of 1 square foot of vent area for every 150 square feet of attic space
- The size and placement of the soffit vents should be coordinated with the size and placement of the exhaust vents to create a balanced ventilation system
- Soffit vents should be kept clear of insulation and other obstructions to ensure proper airflow

## 3. Gable Vents

Gable vents are installed in the gable ends of the roof, where they allow warm, moist air to escape from the attic space. They are a popular choice for homes with a simple gable roof design, and can be used in conjunction with soffit vents to create a balanced ventilation system.

Advantages of gable vents:
- Provide an effective means of exhaust ventilation for homes with a gable roof design

- Can be installed in a variety of sizes and styles to suit the specific needs of your home
- Are relatively easy to install and maintain compared to other types of vents

Installation considerations:
- Gable vents should be sized and positioned to provide adequate ventilation for the attic space, with a minimum of 1 square foot of vent area for every 300 square feet of attic space
- The placement of the gable vents should be coordinated with the placement of the soffit vents to create a balanced ventilation system
- Gable vents should be equipped with screens or louvers to prevent the entry of pests and debris

**Selecting the Right Vents for Your Home**
When selecting the right vents for your home, there are several key factors to consider, including:

1. The size and configuration of your roof
   The type and placement of vents will depend on the size, shape, and slope of your roof, as well as the size and layout of your attic space

2. The climate and weather conditions in your area
   The type and capacity of vents needed will vary depending on factors such as temperature, humidity, and wind exposure

3. The ventilation requirements of your home
   The size and number of vents needed will depend on factors such as the size of your attic space, the amount of insulation, and the number of occupants in your home

4. The aesthetics of your home

 The style and placement of vents should be chosen to complement the overall appearance of your home and to minimize their visual impact

To ensure that you select and install the right vents for your home, it's important to consult with a qualified roofing contractor or ventilation specialist. They can help you assess your specific needs and recommend a ventilation system that will provide optimal performance and durability over time.

## Installing and Maintaining Your Ventilation System

Once you've selected the right vents for your home, it's important to ensure that they are installed and maintained correctly to ensure optimal performance. Some key steps for installing and maintaining your ventilation system include:

1. Follow manufacturer's instructions

 When installing vents, be sure to follow the manufacturer's instructions carefully, including guidelines for sizing, spacing, and positioning of the vents

2. Use high-quality materials

 Use high-quality, durable materials that are designed specifically for use in roof ventilation systems, such as corrosion-resistant fasteners and weatherproof sealants

3. Ensure proper balance and airflow

 When installing a combination of intake and exhaust vents, be sure to balance the size and placement of the vents to ensure proper airflow and prevent pressure imbalances

4. Inspect and maintain regularly

Regularly inspect your ventilation system for signs of damage, blockages, or other issues, and perform routine maintenance such as cleaning and repairs as needed

5. Work with a professional

If you are unsure about any aspect of the installation or maintenance process, don't hesitate to consult with a qualified roofing contractor or ventilation specialist for guidance and support

By selecting the right type of vents for your home, installing them correctly, and maintaining them over time, you can help to ensure that your roof ventilation system provides optimal performance and protection for your home. A well-designed and properly maintained ventilation system can help to regulate temperature and moisture levels, improve energy efficiency, and extend the life of your roofing materials, all while creating a healthier and more comfortable living environment for you and your family.

# Installing and Maintaining a Balanced Ventilation System

A balanced ventilation system is essential for ensuring proper airflow and temperature regulation in your attic space. It involves the correct placement and sizing of intake and exhaust vents to create a continuous flow of air that helps to remove excess heat and moisture from your home. In this section, we'll provide a detailed guide on how to install and maintain a balanced ventilation system that will keep your home comfortable, efficient, and protected from damage.

## Installing a Balanced Ventilation System

Step 1: Determine the ventilation requirements for your home
- Calculate the square footage of your attic space and use this to determine the minimum amount of ventilation needed based on local building codes and manufacturer recommendations
- As a general rule, you should have at least 1 square foot of ventilation (both intake and exhaust) for every 300 square feet of attic space

Step 2: Select the appropriate types and sizes of vents
- Choose a combination of intake and exhaust vents that will provide the required amount of ventilation for your home
- For intake vents, options include soffit vents, eave vents, and gable vents
- For exhaust vents, options include ridge vents, box vents, and power vents
- Consider factors such as the size and shape of your roof, the climate in your area, and the aesthetics of your home when selecting vents

Step 3: Install the intake vents
- For soffit vents, cut a continuous strip of vents along the underside of the eaves, ensuring that the vents are sized and spaced appropriately for your ventilation needs
- For eave vents, cut a series of holes along the underside of the eaves and install individual vent units in each hole
- For gable vents, cut a hole in the gable end of the attic and install a vent unit that is sized appropriately for your ventilation needs

Step 4: Install the exhaust vents
- For ridge vents, cut a continuous slot along the peak of the roof and install a vent unit that runs the entire length of the ridge
- For box vents, cut a hole in the roof deck near the peak of the roof and install a vent unit that is sized appropriately for your ventilation needs
- For power vents, cut a hole in the roof deck and install a motorized vent unit that is connected to a thermostat or humidistat to automatically regulate ventilation based on temperature and humidity levels

Step 5: Ensure proper insulation and airflow
- Install baffles or rafter vents along the underside of the roof deck to maintain a clear airflow path from the soffit vents to the ridge vents
- Ensure that the attic insulation is installed correctly and does not block the flow of air through the vents
- Use a combination of batt insulation and loose-fill insulation to achieve the recommended R-value for your climate zone

Step 6: Test and adjust the system
- Once the ventilation system is installed, test it to ensure that it is functioning properly and providing adequate airflow

- Use a smoke pencil or other tool to check for air movement through the vents and identify any areas of blockage or inadequate flow
- Adjust the placement or sizing of the vents as needed to achieve optimal performance

## Maintaining a Balanced Ventilation System

Step 1: Inspect the vents regularly
- Check the intake and exhaust vents at least twice a year (spring and fall) to ensure that they are clear of debris and functioning properly
- Look for signs of damage, such as cracks, gaps, or missing vent covers, and repair or replace as needed

Step 2: Clean the vents as needed
- Use a brush or vacuum to remove any dirt, dust, or debris that may accumulate on the vent covers or inside the vent openings
- For power vents, follow the manufacturer's instructions for cleaning the motor and other components to ensure optimal performance

Step 3: Monitor the attic conditions
- Use a thermometer and hygrometer to regularly check the temperature and humidity levels in your attic space
- Look for signs of moisture buildup, such as condensation on the underside of the roof deck or mold growth on the insulation
- If you notice any issues, adjust the ventilation system or consult with a professional to identify and address the underlying cause

Step 4: Maintain the insulation
- Inspect the attic insulation regularly to ensure that it is in good condition and properly installed
- Replace any damaged or compressed insulation to maintain the recommended R-value and prevent air leaks
- Use a combination of batt insulation and loose-fill insulation to achieve optimal coverage and performance

Step 5: Schedule professional inspections
- Have your ventilation system inspected by a qualified roofing contractor or home inspector at least once every few years
- They can identify any issues with the vents, insulation, or overall system balance and recommend any necessary repairs or upgrades

By following these steps for installing and maintaining a balanced ventilation system, you can help to ensure that your home remains comfortable, efficient, and protected from moisture damage. A well-designed and properly maintained ventilation system is an essential component of a healthy and long-lasting roofing system, and can provide significant benefits for your home and family over time.

Remember to always prioritize safety when working on your roof or in your attic space, and consult with a professional if you are unsure about any aspect of the installation or maintenance process. With the right approach and regular care, your balanced ventilation system can help to keep your home in top condition for years to come.

# Chapter 6
# Leak Prevention and Repair
## Common Causes of Roof Leaks

Roof leaks can cause significant damage to your home's interior, leading to costly repairs and potential health hazards. Understanding the common causes of roof leaks is essential for effective leak prevention and timely repair. In this section, we'll explore the most frequent culprits behind roof leaks and provide insights into how these issues can be addressed.

### 1. Age and Wear
- As roofing materials age, they become more susceptible to deterioration and damage, increasing the likelihood of leaks
- Exposure to the elements, such as UV radiation, temperature fluctuations, and moisture, can accelerate the aging process
- Signs of age-related wear include cracked, curled, or missing shingles, as well as brittle or deteriorated flashing

Prevention and repair:
- Schedule regular roof inspections to identify and address age-related issues before they lead to leaks
- Consider replacing your roof if it is approaching or has exceeded its expected lifespan
- When replacing your roof, choose high-quality, durable materials that are suited to your climate and home's specific needs

### 2. Poor Installation
- Improper installation techniques, such as inadequate overlapping of shingles, incorrect nailing, or failure to properly seal flashings, can create vulnerabilities that lead to leaks
- Poor workmanship during initial installation or subsequent repairs can compromise the integrity of your roofing system

Prevention and repair:

- When installing a new roof or making repairs, always work with a reputable, experienced roofing contractor who follows industry best practices
- Ensure that your contractor uses high-quality materials and pays attention to detail during the installation process
- If you suspect that poor installation is the cause of a leak, have a professional assess the issue and make necessary repairs

3. Damage from Severe Weather

- High winds, hail, and heavy rain can cause direct damage to roofing materials, leading to leaks
- Storms can also cause indirect damage, such as downed trees or flying debris that puncture or dislodge shingles and flashing

Prevention and repair:

- After severe weather events, inspect your roof for signs of damage and address any issues promptly
- Consider installing impact-resistant shingles or other protective measures in areas prone to hail or high winds
- Regularly trim trees near your home to reduce the risk of damage from falling limbs

4. Clogged Gutters and Downspouts

- When gutters and downspouts become clogged with debris, water can overflow and seep under shingles or through vulnerable points in the roofing system
- Standing water in clogged gutters can also cause damage to fascia boards and roof decking

Prevention and repair:

- Clean your gutters and downspouts at least twice a year, or more frequently if you have many trees near your home
- Consider installing gutter guards or covers to prevent debris buildup

- Ensure that downspouts direct water away from your home's foundation to prevent moisture-related issues

5. Inadequate Ventilation
- Poor attic ventilation can lead to moisture buildup, which can cause damage to roofing materials and create leaks
- Excess heat and humidity in the attic can also lead to ice dams in colder climates, which can cause water to back up under shingles

Prevention and repair:
- Ensure that your attic has a balanced ventilation system with adequate intake and exhaust vents
- Maintain proper insulation levels to prevent heat loss and moisture accumulation
- If you suspect that poor ventilation is contributing to leaks, consult with a professional to assess and address the issue

6. Flashing Failures
- Flashing is used to seal areas where the roof meets chimneys, vents, skylights, and other penetrations
- Improperly installed, damaged, or deteriorated flashing can allow water to seep into the roofing system

Prevention and repair:
- Inspect flashing regularly for signs of damage, corrosion, or improper installation
- When making repairs or replacing your roof, ensure that flashing is properly installed and sealed
- Use high-quality, durable flashing materials that are compatible with your roofing system

7. Cracked or Damaged Shingles
- Physical damage to shingles, such as cracks, punctures, or missing granules, can create pathways for water to enter your roofing system
- Damage can be caused by severe weather, foot traffic, or falling debris

Prevention and repair:
- Inspect your roof regularly for signs of shingle damage and address issues promptly
- Avoid walking on your roof whenever possible, and use caution when accessing the roof for maintenance or repairs
- If you need to replace damaged shingles, ensure that the new shingles match the existing ones in size, color, and style

By understanding these common causes of roof leaks and taking proactive steps to prevent and address them, you can help to ensure the longevity and performance of your roofing system. Regular inspections, timely repairs, and proper maintenance are essential for leak prevention and can save you significant time, money, and stress in the long run.

If you suspect a leak in your roof, it's crucial to act quickly to minimize damage and prevent further issues. In the next section, we'll discuss how to locate and repair leaks in your roof, providing step-by-step guidance for addressing this common roofing problem.

# Locating and Repairing Leaks in Your Roof

Discovering a leak in your roof can be a stressful experience, but prompt action can minimize damage and prevent further issues. In this section, we'll provide a comprehensive guide on how to locate and repair leaks in your roof, with step-by-step instructions and valuable tips for a successful outcome.

**Locating the Leak**

Step 1: Identify the signs of a leak
- Look for water stains, discoloration, or sagging on ceilings and walls
- Check for damp or wet insulation in the attic
- Be aware of musty odors or visible mold growth, which can indicate a moisture issue

Step 2: Trace the leak to its source
- Start in the attic, if accessible, and work your way down to the leak's origin
- Use a flashlight to inspect the underside of the roof decking and rafters for signs of water infiltration, such as stains, mold, or wet insulation
- If the leak is not apparent in the attic, examine the roof's exterior for potential entry points, such as damaged shingles, flashing, or vents

Step 3: Conduct a water test (if necessary)
- If the leak's source is not readily apparent, enlist a helper to conduct a water test
- Have the helper systematically spray the roof with a garden hose while you remain inside the attic or upper floor to identify where the water is entering

- Start at the lowest point of the roof and work upward, isolating sections until the leak is located

Step 4: Mark the location of the leak
- Once you've identified the leak's source, mark the spot with a chalk or marker to easily find it when making repairs
- If the leak is in a hard-to-reach area, take photographs or create a detailed diagram to help locate it later

## Repairing the Leak

Step 1: Gather necessary tools and materials
Depending on the type of leak and roofing material, you may need:
- Roofing nails or screws
- Hammer or screwdriver
- Roofing cement or sealant
- Replacement shingles, flashing, or vent boots
- Pry bar and utility knife
- Safety gear (ladder, gloves, non-slip shoes)

Step 2: Repair or replace damaged shingles
- If the leak is caused by a damaged or missing shingle, carefully remove the affected shingle and any remnants of the old roofing cement
- Install a new shingle, ensuring it matches the existing ones in size, color, and style
- Secure the new shingle with roofing nails and apply a bead of roofing cement around the edges to create a watertight seal

Step 3: Fix or replace damaged flashing
- If the leak is caused by damaged or improperly installed flashing, carefully remove the old flashing and clean the area

- Install new flashing that is compatible with your roofing material, ensuring it is properly overlapped and sealed with roofing cement
- For metal flashing, use a metal-to-metal sealant to create a watertight bond

Step 4: Address issues with vents or skylights
- If the leak is around a vent or skylight, check for cracks or gaps in the sealant or flashing
- Clean the area thoroughly and apply fresh roofing cement or sealant to create a watertight seal
- If the vent or skylight is damaged, replace it with a new unit that is compatible with your roofing system

Step 5: Inspect and test the repair
- After completing the repair, conduct a visual inspection to ensure all components are properly installed and sealed
- Use a garden hose to gently spray the repaired area and check for any signs of leaks or water infiltration
- Monitor the repair over the next few rainfall events to ensure it remains watertight

Tips for Successful Leak Repair
- Always prioritize safety when working on your roof, and use proper equipment and techniques
- If you are unsure about any aspect of the repair process or encounter a complex issue, consult with a professional roofing contractor
- After repairing the leak, take proactive steps to prevent future issues, such as maintaining proper ventilation, cleaning gutters and downspouts, and conducting regular roof inspections

By following these steps and tips for locating and repairing leaks in your roof, you can address this common roofing issue and protect your home from water damage. Remember that early detection and prompt action are key to minimizing the impact of a roof leak and preventing more extensive repairs down the line.

In the next section, we'll discuss preventative measures you can take to avoid future leaks and keep your roofing system in top condition for years to come.

# Preventative Measures to Avoid Future Leaks

While locating and repairing leaks is essential for maintaining the integrity of your roofing system, taking preventative measures can help you avoid future leaks altogether. By implementing proactive strategies and performing regular maintenance, you can extend the life of your roof and minimize the risk of water damage to your home. In this section, we'll explore a range of preventative measures you can take to keep your roof leak-free.

1. Schedule Regular Inspections
  - Conduct a thorough roof inspection at least twice a year (spring and fall) and after severe weather events
  - Check for signs of wear, damage, or deterioration, such as cracked or missing shingles, damaged flashing, or loose seams
  - Identify and address any issues promptly to prevent them from developing into leaks
  - Consider hiring a professional roofing contractor for a comprehensive inspection every few years

2. Keep Gutters and Downspouts Clean
  - Clean your gutters and downspouts at least twice a year to prevent debris buildup and ensure proper water flow
  - Remove leaves, twigs, and other debris that can clog gutters and cause water to overflow onto your roof
  - Check for any damage or leaks in the gutter system and repair or replace components as needed
  - Consider installing gutter guards to minimize debris accumulation and reduce maintenance requirements

3. Trim Overhanging Branches
  - Regularly trim any tree branches that overhang your roof to prevent damage from falling limbs or debris

- Ensure there is a minimum 6-foot clearance between your roof and any nearby trees
- Remove any dead, dying, or diseased branches that could pose a risk to your roof during storms or high winds

## 4. Maintain Proper Ventilation
- Ensure your attic has adequate ventilation to regulate temperature and moisture levels
- Install a balanced system of intake and exhaust vents to promote proper airflow and prevent heat and humidity buildup
- Check that vents are clear of obstructions and functioning properly
- Address any ventilation issues promptly to avoid moisture-related damage to your roofing system

## 5. Monitor and Repair Flashing
- Inspect flashing around chimneys, vents, skylights, and other roof penetrations for signs of damage, corrosion, or improper installation
- Repair or replace damaged flashing promptly to prevent water infiltration
- Ensure flashing is properly sealed with roofing cement or sealant and securely fastened to the roof deck
- When replacing your roof, consider upgrading to high-quality, durable flashing materials for added protection

## 6. Maintain Proper Insulation
- Ensure your attic has sufficient insulation to prevent heat loss and minimize the risk of ice dams in colder climates
- Check that insulation is evenly distributed and not blocking ventilation pathways
- Replace any damaged or moisture-laden insulation to maintain its effectiveness

- Consider adding insulation to improve energy efficiency and reduce the workload on your roofing system

7. Address Drainage Issues
- Ensure that your roof has proper drainage to prevent water from pooling or accumulating on its surface
- Check that the roof slope is adequate for your climate and roofing material
- Install crickets or diverters to direct water away from chimneys, skylights, or other potential leak-prone areas
- Address any drainage issues in your landscaping that could direct water towards your home's foundation

8. Avoid Pressure Washing
- Refrain from pressure washing your roof, as the high-pressure water can damage shingles and force water under the roofing material
- If your roof requires cleaning, use a gentle, low-pressure method, such as a soft-bristled brush or a specialized roof cleaning solution
- Consider hiring a professional roof cleaning service with experience in safe, effective techniques

9. Be Cautious with Roof Traffic
- Minimize foot traffic on your roof to avoid damaging shingles or other roofing components
- When accessing your roof for maintenance or repairs, use caution and follow proper safety protocols
- Place ladders and other equipment carefully to avoid causing damage to the roof surface
- If you require frequent roof access, consider installing a designated walkway or using protective mats to minimize wear and tear

10. Choose Quality Materials and Installation
- When installing a new roof or replacing an old one, invest in high-quality, durable roofing materials that are suitable for your climate and home's specific needs
- Research and compare different roofing options to find the best combination of performance, longevity, and cost-effectiveness
- Always work with a reputable, experienced roofing contractor who follows industry best practices and provides a warranty on their workmanship
- Ensure proper installation techniques are followed, including adequate overlapping, secure fastening, and proper sealing of all components

By implementing these preventative measures and making roof maintenance a regular part of your home upkeep routine, you can significantly reduce the risk of leaks and extend the lifespan of your roofing system. Remember that small investments in prevention and early intervention can save you significant time, money, and stress in the long run.

In the next section, we'll discuss seasonal roofing concerns and provide guidance on how to prepare your roof for the unique challenges of winter weather and summer heat.

# Chapter 7
# Seasonal Roofing Concerns
## Preparing Your Roof for Winter Weather

As the seasons change, your roof faces different challenges and potential issues. Winter weather, in particular, can be harsh on your roofing system, with freezing temperatures, heavy snowfall, and the formation of ice dams all posing risks to its integrity. In this section, we'll discuss how to prepare your roof for the winter months and minimize the likelihood of damage or leaks.

1. Conduct a Pre-Winter Inspection
   - Schedule a thorough roof inspection in the fall, before winter weather sets in
   - Check for any signs of damage, wear, or deterioration that could worsen under the stress of winter conditions
   - Look for cracked, missing, or loose shingles, damaged flashing, or sagging roof decking
   - Identify and address any issues promptly to ensure your roof is in optimal condition before the first snowfall

2. Clean and Repair Gutters and Downspouts
   - Remove any debris, such as leaves or twigs, that has accumulated in your gutters and downspouts
   - Check for any leaks, cracks, or other damage to the gutter system and repair or replace components as needed
   - Ensure gutters and downspouts are securely fastened to your home and directed away from the foundation
   - Consider installing gutter guards to prevent debris buildup and ice formation during the winter months

## 3. Trim Overhanging Branches

- Cut back any tree branches that overhang your roof or are in close proximity to your home
- Remove any dead, dying, or diseased limbs that could break under the weight of snow and ice
- Ensure there is a minimum 6-foot clearance between your roof and any nearby trees to minimize the risk of damage

## 4. Ensure Proper Attic Ventilation and Insulation

- Check that your attic has adequate ventilation to regulate temperature and moisture levels during the winter months
- Ensure vents are clear of obstructions and functioning properly to allow for proper airflow
- Inspect your attic insulation to ensure it is evenly distributed and providing sufficient thermal protection
- Address any ventilation or insulation issues promptly to prevent heat loss and the formation of ice dams

## 5. Prevent Ice Dams

- Ice dams form when heat from the attic melts snow on the roof, which then refreezes at the colder eaves, creating a dam that prevents proper drainage
- To prevent ice dams, maintain proper attic ventilation and insulation to keep the roof deck at a consistent temperature
- Consider installing heating cables along the eaves and in gutters to melt snow and ice and promote proper drainage
- Use a roof rake to remove snow from the lower portion of the roof, reducing the risk of ice dam formation

## 6. Monitor Snow Accumulation

- Keep an eye on snow accumulation on your roof throughout the winter months
- Use a roof rake to remove excess snow, especially if your roof has a low slope or is prone to ice dams

- Avoid using metal shovels or sharp tools that could damage your roofing material
- If you have a flat or low-slope roof, consider hiring a professional snow removal service to safely clear heavy snowfall

## 7. Check for Signs of Stress or Damage
- During and after winter storms, inspect your roof and attic for any signs of stress or damage
- Look for sagging or bowing of the roof deck, which could indicate excessive snow load
- Check for any new leaks or water stains on ceilings or walls, which could signal ice dam formation or other winter-related issues
- Address any concerns promptly to prevent further damage and ensure the continued protection of your home

## 8. Schedule a Professional Post-Winter Inspection
- Once winter weather has subsided, schedule a professional roof inspection to assess the condition of your roofing system
- A qualified roofing contractor can identify any issues that may have developed over the winter months and recommend appropriate repairs or maintenance
- Addressing winter-related damage early can prevent more extensive and costly issues down the line

By taking these proactive steps to prepare your roof for winter weather, you can minimize the risk of leaks, damage, and other cold-weather concerns. Remember that regular maintenance and timely repairs are essential for ensuring the longevity and performance of your roofing system, no matter the season.

In the next section, we'll explore the unique challenges that summer weather poses for your roof and provide guidance on how to address issues like heat damage, UV degradation, and storm-related concerns.

# Addressing Ice Dams and Snow Buildup

Ice dams and excessive snow buildup are two of the most common and potentially damaging winter roofing concerns. When left unaddressed, these issues can lead to leaks, structural damage, and premature deterioration of your roofing system. In this section, we'll take a closer look at how ice dams and snow buildup form, the risks they pose, and the steps you can take to prevent and address these winter weather challenges.

Understanding Ice Dams
- Ice dams form when heat from the attic melts snow on the upper portion of the roof, causing water to run down to the colder eaves, where it refreezes
- As this process repeats, the ice buildup at the eaves creates a dam that prevents proper drainage, forcing water to back up under the shingles and into the attic or living spaces
- Common signs of ice dams include icicles hanging from the eaves, water stains on ceilings or walls, and the presence of ice or water on the exterior walls

Risks of Ice Dams
Water infiltration caused by ice dams can lead to a range of problems, including:
- Damage to insulation, drywall, and other interior finishes
- Mold and mildew growth, which can pose health risks and compromise indoor air quality
- Structural damage to rafters, decking, and other roofing components
- Premature deterioration of shingles and flashing due to prolonged exposure to moisture
- In addition to the direct damage caused by water infiltration, the weight of ice dams can place excessive stress on gutters and eaves, potentially leading to sagging, separation, or collapse.

**Preventing Ice Dams**

1. Ensure proper attic ventilation
   - Maintain a balanced system of intake and exhaust vents to promote proper airflow and regulate attic temperature
   - Keep vents clear of obstructions, such as insulation or debris, to ensure optimal performance
2. Improve attic insulation
   - Install adequate insulation to prevent heat loss from the living space into the attic
   - Ensure insulation is evenly distributed and maintains a consistent R-value across the attic floor
   - Pay special attention to areas around recessed lighting, chimneys, and other penetrations
3. Seal air leaks
   - Identify and seal any air leaks between the living space and the attic, such as gaps around pipes, ducts, or electrical wiring
   - Use weatherstripping, caulk, or expanding foam to create an airtight barrier and prevent warm air from entering the attic
4. Install heating cables
   - Consider installing electric heating cables along the eaves and in gutters to melt snow and ice and promote proper drainage
   - Follow manufacturer guidelines for installation and operation, and use caution to avoid overloading electrical circuits
5. Remove snow from the roof
   - Use a roof rake to remove snow from the lower portion of the roof, reducing the risk of ice dam formation
   - Avoid using metal shovels or sharp tools that could damage your roofing material
   - Consider hiring a professional snow removal service for heavy snowfall or hard-to-reach areas

Addressing Snow Buildup
- While a moderate amount of snow on your roof is generally not a concern, excessive snow buildup can place significant stress on your roofing system

- The weight of snow and ice can cause the roof deck to sag or bow, potentially leading to structural damage or collapse
- In addition, heavy snow buildup can exacerbate the formation of ice dams and increase the risk of water infiltration

Signs of Excessive Snow Load
- Sagging or bowing of the roof deck, visible from the attic or exterior of the home
- Cracks in the drywall or plaster of interior walls and ceilings
- Doors and windows that suddenly become difficult to open or close
- Unusual creaking, cracking, or popping sounds coming from the roof or attic

## Removing Snow from Your Roof
1. Use a roof rake
- A roof rake with an extended handle allows you to safely remove snow from the ground or a ladder
- Start at the eaves and work your way up the roof, taking care not to damage shingles or other roofing components
2. Hire a professional snow removal service
- For heavy snowfall, high roofs, or complex roof designs, it's often best to hire a professional snow removal service
- Look for a contractor with experience in safe and effective snow removal techniques, and ensure they have proper insurance coverage
3. Avoid using salt or chemical deicers
- While salt and chemical deicers can help melt snow and ice, they can also damage your roofing material and cause corrosion to metal components
- If you must use a deicer, opt for a non-corrosive, roof-safe product and apply it sparingly

By understanding the risks of ice dams and snow buildup and taking proactive steps to prevent and address these winter roofing concerns, you can help protect your home from the damaging effects of harsh winter weather. Regular inspections, timely maintenance, and prompt action when issues arise are key to ensuring the longevity and performance of your roofing system.

In the next section, we'll explore the unique challenges that summer weather poses for your roof, including heat damage, UV degradation, and storm-related concerns, and provide guidance on how to keep your roof in top condition during the warmer months

# Summer Roofing Challenges: Heat, UV Rays, and Storms

While winter weather can be harsh on your roofing system, summer brings its own set of challenges that can lead to damage, premature aging, and reduced performance. In this section, we'll discuss the primary summer roofing concerns, including heat, UV rays, and storms, and provide guidance on how to protect your roof and ensure its longevity.

### Heat-Related Concerns

1. Thermal shock
   - Thermal shock occurs when your roof experiences rapid temperature changes, such as during a summer thunderstorm when cool rain falls on a hot roof
   - These sudden temperature fluctuations can cause roofing materials to expand and contract, leading to cracking, splitting, or warping
   - To minimize the risk of thermal shock, choose roofing materials with high thermal stability and ensure proper attic ventilation to regulate roof temperature

2. Accelerated aging
   - High temperatures can accelerate the aging process of roofing materials, particularly asphalt shingles
   - Prolonged exposure to heat can cause shingles to become brittle, crack, or curl, reducing their effectiveness and lifespan
   - To combat heat-related aging, consider installing a light-colored or reflective roof that minimizes heat absorption, and ensure proper ventilation to dissipate heat from the attic

3. Softening and warping
   - Extreme heat can cause some roofing materials, such as asphalt shingles or PVC membranes, to soften and become more susceptible to damage

- Softened materials may be more prone to punctures, tears, or indentations, especially in areas with high foot traffic or falling debris
- To prevent heat-related softening and warping, choose roofing materials with high heat resistance and avoid walking on the roof during the hottest parts of the day

## UV Radiation Concerns

1. Material degradation
   - Ultraviolet (UV) radiation from the sun can break down the chemical bonds in roofing materials, leading to premature aging and deterioration
   - This degradation can manifest as cracking, fading, or loss of granules in asphalt shingles, or chalking and discoloration in metal roofs
   - To minimize UV damage, choose roofing materials with high UV resistance, such as shingles with UV-reflective granules or metal roofs with protective coatings
2. Sealant and adhesive failure
   - UV radiation can also degrade the sealants and adhesives used in roofing systems, compromising their ability to prevent leaks and maintain a watertight seal
   - This can lead to gaps or voids around flashing, vents, or other penetrations, allowing water to enter the roofing system
   - To prevent UV-related sealant and adhesive failure, choose high-quality, UV-resistant products and inspect and maintain these components regularly
3. Fading and discoloration
   - Prolonged exposure to UV rays can cause roofing materials to fade or discolor, detracting from the aesthetic appeal of your home
   - While this may not directly impact the performance of your roof, it can affect your home's curb appeal and resale value

- To minimize fading and discoloration, choose roofing materials with high color stability and consider applying a UV-resistant coating or sealant to protect the surface

## Storm-Related Concerns

1. High winds
   - Strong winds associated with summer storms can cause shingles to lift, tear, or blow off entirely, leaving your roof vulnerable to leaks and water damage
   - Wind-driven debris, such as tree branches or outdoor furniture, can also impact your roof, causing punctures or other damage
   - To protect your roof from wind damage, ensure shingles are properly secured and consider installing a wind-resistant roofing system in high-wind areas
2. Hail damage
   - Hailstorms can cause significant damage to roofing materials, leaving dents, cracks, or even holes in shingles, metal panels, or tiles
   - Hail damage can compromise the integrity of your roofing system, leading to leaks and water infiltration
   - To minimize the risk of hail damage, consider installing impact-resistant roofing materials, such as modified asphalt shingles or metal roofs with high impact ratings
3. Lightning strikes
   - While relatively rare, lightning strikes can cause severe damage to your roofing system, including fires, structural damage, and electrical issues
   - Lightning can also damage roof-mounted equipment, such as HVAC units or solar panels, compromising their performance and safety
   - To protect your roof from lightning strikes, consider installing a lightning protection system, which includes air terminals, conductors, and grounding electrodes to safely divert lightning energy away from your home

## Protecting Your Roof from Summer Challenges

1. Schedule regular inspections
   - Have your roof inspected by a professional at least once a year, ideally before and after the summer season
   - Identify and address any issues related to heat, UV radiation, or storm damage promptly to prevent further deterioration
2. Perform routine maintenance
   - Keep your roof clean and free of debris, such as leaves, twigs, or moss, which can trap moisture and promote degradation
   - Ensure gutters and downspouts are clear and functioning properly to prevent water from backing up onto the roof
   - Trim overhanging tree branches to minimize the risk of damage from falling limbs or wind-blown debris
3. Invest in preventative measures
   - Consider installing a reflective or light-colored roof to minimize heat absorption and reduce cooling costs
   - Choose roofing materials with high resistance to UV radiation, heat, and impact damage
   - Ensure proper attic ventilation to regulate roof temperature and prevent premature aging
4. Address storm damage promptly
   - After a severe storm, inspect your roof for signs of wind, hail, or lightning damage
   - Contact a professional roofing contractor to assess the extent of the damage and recommend appropriate repairs
   - File an insurance claim if necessary, and work with your contractor to ensure proper documentation and timely restoration

By understanding the unique challenges that summer weather poses for your roofing system and taking proactive steps to prevent and address heat, UV radiation, and storm-related concerns, you can help extend the life of your roof and ensure its optimal performance. Regular inspections, timely maintenance, and a focus on prevention are key to protecting your home and minimizing the risk of costly repairs or premature replacement.

In the next section, we'll discuss the importance of roofing safety and best practices, including essential safety gear, proper ladder usage, and guidelines for maintaining a safe, stable work environment when installing, repairing, or inspecting your roof.

# Chapter 8
# Roofing Safety and Best Practices
## Essential Safety Gear for Roofing Work

Roofing work can be inherently dangerous, with falls being the leading cause of injuries and fatalities in the construction industry. Whether you're a professional roofing contractor or a homeowner attempting a DIY repair, prioritizing safety is crucial to preventing accidents and ensuring a successful project. In this section, we'll discuss the essential safety gear for roofing work and the importance of using proper equipment and techniques.

### 1. Fall Protection Equipment
Fall protection equipment is the most critical safety gear for roofing work, as it helps prevent serious injuries or fatalities from falls

There are several types of fall protection equipment, including:

a. Personal Fall Arrest System (PFAS)
- Consists of an anchor point, connectors, and a full-body harness
- Designed to stop a fall and distribute the force of impact across the body
- Must be properly fitted and inspected before each use

b. Guardrails
- Provide a barrier along the edge of the roof to prevent falls
- Should be securely attached to the roof deck and meet OSHA height and strength requirements

c. Safety Nets
- Installed below the work area to catch falling workers or debris
- Must be properly sized, positioned, and maintained to ensure effectiveness

- When using fall protection equipment, always follow the manufacturer's instructions and OSHA guidelines for installation, use, and maintenance

## 2. Hard Hats
- Hard hats protect against head injuries from falling objects, low overhead hazards, and accidental impacts
- Choose a hard hat that meets ANSI Z89.1 standards and is appropriate for the specific work environment
- Inspect the hard hat before each use for signs of damage, such as cracks, dents, or excessive wear
- Replace hard hats that have sustained an impact or are beyond their recommended service life

## 3. Non-Slip Footwear
- Proper footwear is essential for maintaining traction and stability on the roof surface
- Choose boots or shoes with slip-resistant soles, such as those with a tread pattern designed for roofing work
- Ensure footwear is in good condition and provides adequate support and protection for the feet and ankles
- Avoid wearing sandals, flip-flops, or other open-toed shoes while working on the roof

## 4. Eye and Face Protection
- Eye and face protection, such as safety glasses or face shields, help prevent injuries from flying debris, dust, or chemicals
- Choose eye and face protection that meets ANSI Z87.1 standards and is appropriate for the specific work environment
- Ensure proper fit and comfort to prevent fogging or slipping during use
- Replace eye and face protection that is scratched, cracked, or otherwise damaged

## 5. Gloves

- Gloves protect the hands from cuts, abrasions, splinters, and other hazards associated with roofing work
- Choose gloves that are appropriate for the specific task and materials being used
- Ensure gloves fit properly and allow for adequate dexterity and grip
- Replace gloves that are worn, torn, or otherwise damaged

## 6. Respirators

- Respirators may be necessary when working with certain roofing materials, such as asphalt or silica dust, to prevent inhalation of harmful particles
- Choose a respirator that is appropriate for the specific hazard and meets NIOSH approval standards
- Ensure proper fit and seal to prevent leakage around the edges
- Follow the manufacturer's instructions for use, maintenance, and replacement

## 7. High-Visibility Clothing

- High-visibility clothing, such as vests or shirts, helps make workers more visible to others on the job site
- Choose high-visibility clothing that meets ANSI/ISEA 107 standards and is appropriate for the specific work environment
- Ensure clothing is clean and in good condition to maintain its reflective properties
- Replace high-visibility clothing that is faded, torn, or otherwise damaged

## Best Practices for Safe Roofing Work

### 1. Proper Training and Supervision

- Ensure all workers are properly trained in fall protection, equipment use, and emergency procedures
- Provide ongoing supervision and guidance to ensure compliance with safety protocols

2. Hazard Assessment and Planning
- Conduct a thorough hazard assessment of the work area before beginning any roofing work
- Develop a site-specific safety plan that addresses identified hazards and outlines appropriate control measures

3. Equipment Inspection and Maintenance
- Regularly inspect all safety gear and equipment for signs of wear, damage, or malfunction
- Follow the manufacturer's instructions for maintenance, storage, and replacement

4. Proper Ladder Usage
- Choose the appropriate ladder for the specific task and work environment
- Ensure ladders are in good condition and free of defects
- Set up ladders on a stable, level surface and secure them to prevent slipping or shifting

5. Weather Awareness
- Monitor weather conditions and postpone work during severe storms, high winds, or extreme temperatures
- Use caution when working on wet or icy surfaces, and ensure proper slip protection is in place

6. Hydration and Sun Protection
- Encourage workers to stay hydrated and take regular breaks to prevent heat stress and fatigue
- Provide and encourage the use of sunscreen, hats, and other sun protection measures to prevent skin damage

7. Communication and Emergency Planning
- Establish clear communication protocols among workers and with supervisors
- Develop an emergency action plan that outlines procedures for responding to accidents, injuries, or other incidents
- Ensure all workers are familiar with the emergency action plan and know how to summon help if needed

By using the essential safety gear and following best practices for safe roofing work, you can significantly reduce the risk of accidents and injuries on the job site. Remember, safety should always be the top priority when working on a roof, regardless of the scope or complexity of the project.

In the final section, we'll summarize the key points covered throughout this guide and emphasize the importance of regular maintenance, timely repairs, and professional guidance in ensuring the longevity and performance of your roofing system.

# Ladder Safety and Proper Roof Navigation

Ladders are an essential tool for accessing your roof, but they can also be a significant safety hazard if used improperly. Falls from ladders account for a high number of roofing-related injuries and fatalities each year. Similarly, navigating a roof safely requires an understanding of proper techniques and potential hazards. In this section, we'll discuss ladder safety and proper roof navigation to help you maintain a safe, stable work environment when installing, repairing, or inspecting your roof.

## Ladder Safety

1. Choosing the Right Ladder
- Select a ladder that is appropriate for the specific task and work environment
- Consider factors such as the ladder's weight capacity, height, and material (e.g., aluminum, fiberglass, or wood)
- Ensure the ladder is in good condition and free of defects, such as bent or missing rungs, cracks, or corrosion

2. Setting Up the Ladder
- Place the ladder on a stable, level surface, avoiding soft ground, ice, or wet surfaces
- Ensure the ladder is set at the proper angle (75 degrees or a 4:1 ratio of height to base distance)
- Extend the ladder at least 3 feet above the roofline or landing platform to provide a handhold for getting on and off the roof
- Secure the ladder at the top and bottom to prevent slipping or shifting during use

3. Climbing and Descending
- Face the ladder when climbing or descending, maintaining three points of contact (two hands and one foot, or two feet and one hand) at all times

- Keep your body centered between the side rails, avoiding overreaching or leaning too far to one side
- Avoid carrying heavy or bulky items while climbing the ladder; use a tool belt, rope, or hoist to bring materials up to the roof
- Do not allow more than one person on the ladder at a time, unless the ladder is specifically designed for multiple users

4. Maintenance and Inspection
- Regularly inspect ladders for signs of wear, damage, or defects, such as bent or missing rungs, cracks, or corrosion
- Clean ladders after each use to remove dirt, debris, or chemicals that may deteriorate the material over time
- Store ladders in a safe, dry location away from heat sources or direct sunlight
- Follow the manufacturer's instructions for maintenance, repair, and replacement of ladders

## Proper Roof Navigation

1. Assessing the Roof Condition
- Before navigating the roof, conduct a visual inspection from the ground or a ladder to identify potential hazards, such as loose or missing shingles, soft spots, or exposed nails
- Take note of the roof pitch, material, and any obstacles or protrusions that may affect your footing or balance
- If the roof appears to be in poor condition or you are unsure about its stability, consider hiring a professional roofing contractor to perform the work

2. Using Proper Footwear
- Wear shoes or boots with slip-resistant soles, such as those with a tread pattern designed for roofing work
- Ensure footwear is in good condition and provides adequate support and protection for the feet and ankles
- Avoid wearing sandals, flip-flops, or other open-toed shoes while navigating the roof

3. Maintaining Balance and Stability
- Use a roof harness or other fall protection equipment when working on steep or slippery surfaces
- Keep your center of gravity low and your feet shoulder-width apart to maintain balance
- Avoid walking on wet, icy, or debris-covered surfaces, which can increase the risk of slips and falls
- Use a roof rake or broom to remove loose debris or snow before navigating the roof

4. Navigating Around Obstacles and Openings
- Be aware of skylights, vents, chimneys, and other protrusions that may pose tripping hazards or weak spots in the roof surface
- Maintain a safe distance from the edge of the roof, using a chalk line or other visual marker to delineate a safe working area
- Use caution when navigating around roof valleys, hips, and ridges, as these areas may have a steeper pitch or uneven surface
- Cover or guard any openings or holes in the roof surface to prevent falls or accidents

5. Working in Teams
- When possible, work in teams of two or more people when navigating the roof
- Establish clear communication protocols and use visual or audible signals to alert others of potential hazards or emergencies
- Ensure each team member is properly trained in fall protection, emergency response, and other safety procedures
- Have a designated spotter on the ground to monitor the work area and summon help if needed

By following these guidelines for ladder safety and proper roof navigation, you can significantly reduce the risk of accidents and injuries when working on your roof. Remember, safety should always be the top priority, and if you are unsure about your ability to navigate the roof safely, it is best to hire a professional roofing contractor to perform the work.

Regular maintenance and inspection of your ladder and fall protection equipment, as well as a thorough assessment of the roof condition before each use, can help ensure a safe and stable work environment. By prioritizing safety and using proper techniques, you can confidently tackle your roofing projects while minimizing the risk of harm to yourself and others.

# Best Practices for a Long-Lasting, Trouble-Free Roof

A long-lasting, trouble-free roof is the result of a combination of proper installation, regular maintenance, and timely repairs. By following best practices in each of these areas, you can maximize the lifespan of your roofing system and minimize the risk of leaks, damage, and premature failure. In this section, we'll discuss the key steps you can take to ensure your roof remains in top condition for years to come.

1. Proper Installation
- Choose a reputable, experienced roofing contractor who is licensed, insured, and follows industry best practices
- Select high-quality roofing materials that are appropriate for your climate, building type, and aesthetic preferences
- Ensure the roof deck is properly prepared, with any damaged or rotted wood replaced and the surface cleaned and smoothed
- Install a suitable underlayment, such as felt paper or synthetic membrane, to provide an additional layer of protection against water infiltration
- Use proper flashing techniques around chimneys, vents, skylights, and other penetrations to prevent leaks and moisture damage
- Ensure adequate ventilation in the attic space to regulate temperature and moisture levels and prevent premature aging of roofing materials
- Follow the manufacturer's instructions for installation, including proper nail placement, overlapping of shingles, and sealing of seams and edges

2. Regular Maintenance
- Conduct a visual inspection of your roof at least twice a year, in the spring and fall, to identify any signs of damage, wear, or deterioration

- Check for missing, cracked, or curling shingles, as well as any bare spots or areas of granule loss
- Look for signs of moisture damage, such as water stains on the ceiling or walls, or the presence of mold or mildew in the attic
- Clean gutters and downspouts regularly to prevent clogs and ensure proper drainage away from the foundation
- Trim overhanging tree branches to reduce the risk of damage from falling limbs or debris accumulation on the roof surface
- Remove any moss, algae, or lichen growth using a soft-bristled brush or specialized cleaning solution to prevent moisture retention and shingle deterioration
- Ensure proper ventilation in the attic space, with a balance of intake and exhaust vents to regulate temperature and moisture levels
- Schedule professional inspections every 2-3 years, or more frequently if recommended by your roofing contractor, to identify and address any hidden or developing issues

3. Timely Repairs
- Address any signs of damage or deterioration promptly to prevent further harm to your roofing system
- Replace missing, cracked, or severely curled shingles as soon as possible to maintain the integrity of the roof surface
- Repair or replace damaged flashing around chimneys, vents, skylights, and other penetrations to prevent leaks and moisture infiltration
- Address any signs of moisture damage in the attic, such as wet insulation or water stains, to prevent the growth of mold and mildew and protect the structural integrity of your home
- If you notice any signs of sagging, unevenness, or instability in the roof surface, contact a professional roofing contractor immediately to assess the extent of the damage and recommend appropriate repairs

- Consider upgrading to more durable, weather-resistant roofing materials when making repairs or replacements to enhance the longevity and performance of your roofing system

## 4. Proactive Measures
- Install gutter guards or covers to prevent debris accumulation and minimize the need for frequent cleaning
- Consider applying a roof coating or sealant to protect against UV damage, moisture infiltration, and premature aging of roofing materials
- Invest in regular professional maintenance and cleaning services to keep your roof in optimal condition and identify potential issues early on
- Educate yourself on the signs of roof damage and deterioration, and take action promptly when any concerns arise
- Keep accurate records of all roofing installations, repairs, and maintenance activities to facilitate warranty claims and future reference

By following these best practices for proper installation, regular maintenance, timely repairs, and proactive measures, you can significantly extend the lifespan of your roofing system and minimize the risk of costly damage or premature failure. A well-maintained roof not only protects your home and its occupants from the elements but also enhances its energy efficiency, curb appeal, and overall value.

Remember, the key to a long-lasting, trouble-free roof is a commitment to ongoing care and attention. By partnering with a trusted roofing contractor and taking an active role in the maintenance and repair of your roofing system, you can enjoy the peace of mind that comes with knowing your home is well-protected for years to come.

# Conclusion

Throughout this comprehensive guide, we've explored the essential aspects of roofing installation, repair, and maintenance. From understanding the different types of roofing materials and their unique benefits to mastering the art of leak prevention and weatherproofing, you now have the knowledge and tools to ensure your roof remains a reliable, protective barrier for your home.

As we've discussed, a well-maintained roof is crucial not only for the structural integrity of your home but also for the safety, comfort, and well-being of you and your family. By investing time and effort into regular inspections, timely repairs, and proactive maintenance, you can extend the lifespan of your roofing system, minimize the risk of costly damage, and enjoy the peace of mind that comes with a secure, functional roof overhead.

While the task of maintaining a healthy roof may seem daunting at times, remember that you don't have to go it alone. By partnering with a trusted, experienced roofing contractor and staying informed about the latest best practices and industry standards, you can ensure that your roof receives the care and attention it needs to perform at its best.

As you move forward in your roofing journey, keep this guide close at hand as a valuable reference and reminder of the key principles and techniques that underlie a successful roofing project. Whether you're tackling a minor repair or considering a full replacement, the insights and advice contained within these pages will help you make informed decisions and achieve optimal results.

Remember, your roof is your home's first line of defense against the elements, and by treating it with the care and respect it deserves, you can ensure that it continues to provide reliable, long-lasting protection for years to come. So here's to your roofing success, and to the peace of mind that comes with knowing your home is safe, secure, and ready to weather any storm.

Printed in Great Britain
by Amazon

60370180R00067

# How to Install and Repair Roofing

The Ultimate DIY Guide to Roof Repair,
Shingle Replacement, Leak Prevention,
Flashing Installation, and Ventilation
System Maintenance

**The Fix It Guy**

# Copyright © 2024 by The Fix It Guy